Before You Say "I Do"...
TO A MUSLIM

SARAH IBRAHIM

ANM
publishers

Before You Say "I Do"
... TO A MUSLIM

by Sarah Ibrahim

ISBN: 978-0-9794929-9-0 Paperback

Published by:

Advancing Native Missions
P.O. Box 5303 • Charlottesville, VA 22905
www.AdvancingNativeMissions.com

Acknowledgment

There are numerous individuals and close friends to whom I am personally indebted, from the core of my heart, for all the encouragement, prayers, assistance, and sacrificial support they have extended to me while writing this book.

I am much obliged to Mrs. Rosemary, Mrs. Jane, and Mrs. Grannie for all their dedication, enthusiasm, sacrifice, and endless hours in helping to make this book possible.

Lastly, and most importantly, I am most grateful for my husband's and my children's support, understanding, and patience during the whole process of writing and editing.

Dedication

To all women who are enslaved by Muslim men and looking for a hope to flee from the bondage. May they find hope, peace, and joy in knowing the Person of Jesus Christ.

To all the people who have the courage and boldness to speak the truth concerning the mistreatment of Muslim women.

To all believers in Christ who take every opportunity to share the glorious truth and grace of our Lord Jesus Christ to all who are lost and perishing.

Table of Contents

Preface ix

Introduction xiii

1. *Brood of Vipers* 1

2. *Love is Blind, but Marriage is an Eye Opener* 15

3. *Her First Veil* 31

4. *The Obedient Muslim Woman* 57

5. *In the Name of Honor* 73

6. *The Mirage of Afterlife* 89

7. *The Assurance* 109

8. *The Covenant* 119

9. *The Final Answer is?* 131

References 153

Preface

I want to thank God for using me to write this book in an effort to reach those who will suffer at the hands of Muslim men. I feel that it is Christ Himself who has enabled me to take on the task of authoring this book, just as He is the Author of my life.

For more than three years, during the process of writing this book, I went through an extremely difficult time. It is true to say that I was being threatened by great evil. However, I rejoice in knowing that the Lord was by my side, and He has set me free from all of my fears. I can finally say with bold conviction that no matter what I have been through, Christ has been with me every step of the way, strengthening and guiding me.

Let me introduce myself. I am originally from a Muslim country, born and bred in a believing Christian home. After completing my education, I took Ibrahim as my husband in an arranged Christian marriage, as is common for Christians living in most Muslim countries. At that time, I had no idea where the Lord was leading me; I was following my husband as he sought lost souls for Jesus Christ.

In 2003, Ibrahim was forced out of our country because he followed his calling to bring people to the Lord. He was caught receiving two shipments of Bibles and materials for distribution. One of the shipments contained three thousand children's Bibles with images of Christ and His disciples and other Old Testament prophets. The pictures in these books are blasphemous according to Islam. So the shipment was seized, and a case was filed against Ibrahim for violating the Blasphemy Laws, punishable by execution. Fearing for his life, Ibrahim fled the country and was able to enter the United States and find safety. The three Christian colleagues who were working with Ibrahim were martyred by the extremists, paying the ultimate price for bringing Christianity into a Muslim country. What were their crimes? They were simply distributing Christian literature and New Testaments in the marketplace. It is prohibited to evangelize in the Muslim world, and anyone who is caught committing such a crime is imprisoned. According to Islamic Sharia law, he or she may later suffer the death penalty. So Ibrahim was in great danger.

Ibrahim's sudden departure left me alone for almost three years, not knowing when, where, or how I would be able to see him again. It was the greatest trial I have ever experienced in my life as I found myself all alone with three small children, clinging to the only hope that I had: the hope that Christ would see me through this difficult period. I was terrified that I would be thrown in prison in place of my husband and that the Muslims would punish me, since I was considered a third-class citizen, an infidel. I feared the consequences of being an infidel: rape, torture, beatings, and even death.

But God had other plans for my family. Through the prayers of many and through trust in Him, He protected us and finally brought our family back together in 2006. It was the happiest day of my life! However, there was sadness in our hearts because our adopted daughter was unable to come with us, since Islam does not accept the concept of adoption. Though we had obtained all the legal papers from the courts, we were considered only guardians of our daughter. Before coming to the United States, Ibrahim's older sister took responsibility of her, and later her biological parents took custody, while we continued providing for her needs. As her loving guardians, we still keep in constant touch with her. But we did not question God. As we embarked on our new life in America, we submitted to His will and obeyed His commands, knowing that our adopted daughter was safe in His protection.

I was aware that Ibrahim continued to be involved in Christian ministry during our separation, but I had no idea in what capacity the Lord was using him, thinking that he was perhaps teaching and preaching. Now I understand why Ibrahim did not share with me what the Lord was doing through him. We had to be very careful what we said as we talked on the phone or shared emails. We knew that if our conversations were overheard, it could endanger our children and me; the Islamic authorities could harm us for what my husband was doing.

It has now been almost eight years since we came to America. In the beginning, I tried to find a job in an effort to utilize my education. However, it seemed as if every door remained firmly shut, but it is amazing how the Lord orchestrates our lives. I believe that our three-year separation from each other and the difficulties we underwent were not by accident, but rather the Lord was patiently preparing me for something. He had brought me here to stand by my husband's side as he reaches out to Christians in this country. I have learned that I have a gift for explaining and sharing the culture of Islamic women with women in the West. I know that the Lord wants me to open the eyes of young girls, especially here in America, as they are enticed by Muslims who are trying to convert them to Islam.

In this book, I want to reach these young women, as well as their mothers, fathers, sisters, and brothers, to warn them so that they may not become victims of these insidious plots to cause them to walk away from their Christian upbringing and become entangled in dangerous webs of deceit.

Introduction

A wise man once said, "Love is blind, but marriage is an eye opener." As you journey with me through this book, I will seek to unveil the truth regarding what Islam teaches about the role and treatment of women and what the consequences of marriage to a Muslim man can be. Today, many western women are involved in relationships with Muslim men and are not aware of what lies ahead for them. These men mesmerize vulnerable western women with their slippery words but do not tell them what the Qur'an, the holy book of Islam, really says about the relationship between men and women or about marriage. Having been brought up in a Muslim country, I have been able to see firsthand what the life of Muslim women is like. For thirty-five years, I lived in a country where ninety-eight percent of the people are Muslims.

I was raised in a country that follows Islamic rules, suppressing women and their rights. Although my sisters and I grew up in a Christian family, we have all witnessed brutal incidents suffered by Muslim and Christian women who have married Muslim men. Why they suffer is based on Islamic teachings and ideology. The status of women, their marriages, their place in society, and their whole identities are all part of the Islamic way of life. What they can do, as well as what happens to them, is laid down in the Qur'an and in other sayings of Muhammad and can never be changed. Our experience of living in such a society has made my family appreciate the Christian men in our lives even more. When I immigrated to the United States, I was glad to leave behind the Islamic life of restriction, oppression, and fear. I found that it is not the people but rather the ideology that creates monsters out of human beings.

In my home country in the place where I worked, many of my colleagues were very lively by nature. During special events, they would throw parties at their homes, to which I would also be invited. Within the boundaries of their homes, there would be music and dancing and cracking of hilarious, and sometimes risqué, jokes. It always was fun to see how freely everyone chatted and laughed in gatherings which were exclusively for women. However, it was a shock to see how differently they would react when their prophet or holy book was questioned. For example, when the issue of the Danish cartoonist arose in 2005, the same women who had been full of fun and accepting of all their friends now showed a different and vengeful attitude. I, personally, do not think it is right to make fun of anyone's religion, but I was frightened by the reaction of my friends. My colleagues became furious with me, as if I was the one who was to be blamed for the cartoons. They spoke harshly and vengefully, frightening me. I wondered how anyone who seemed to be living a normal happy life could become so vicious when it came to the matter of their religion. They seemed to be full of anger, so unlike the forbearance and mercy taught by the Lord Jesus Christ.

Many of these angry female colleagues, however, had little idea of how their religion affected their human rights. Even in America and Europe, women converting to Islam have little or no idea as to what that entails for them as women. Let me share with you about a young American named Angela who converted to Islam following the terrorist attack on September 11, 2001. I watched her interview on television, and my heart broke when I heard what she had to say. She was excited to explain how she felt after embracing Islam. The sad part was that she claimed that she had traveled to India and the Middle East and had found that the Muslims she met there were different—they were kind, loving, hospitable, and caring. She seemed to disagree with her own people, who, she felt, blamed all Muslims for 9/11. Her conversion to Islam came after only two months of studying the Qur'an because, according to her statements in the interview, she wanted to stand with Muslims. She said that when she was a Catholic, she was told that Islam discriminates against women, but after reading the Qur'an, she felt that it was exactly the opposite.

Angela is one of more than 20,000 American women who convert to Islam every year. Surprisingly, for every man, there are four women in the United States who will convert. My first thought was, "Does she know what she is talking about?" Obviously not! How could she know the Qur'an in depth? The Qur'an available in the West is a milder version of the original Qur'an read in Middle Eastern countries, which is in Arabic. Also, it is hard to imagine that anyone who reads the Qur'an will know everything about it in a few months. I believe that Angela's perception will change when she is given a chance to experience life in a Muslim country and to live among the minorities as she tries to survive under Sharia law. She might be shocked to discover how extensively Sharia controls all of one's life.

Sharia law signifies the entire Islamic way of life based on the laws of Allah, the god of Islam. It deals with laws covering crime, politics, economics, and even personal matters, such as sexual intercourse, hygiene, diet, prayers, etiquette, and fasting. It prescribes punishment for deeds that violate the principles outlined in Sharia and pronounces judgment against those who neglect their social obligations. In Sharia law, rape is dealt with very differently than in the West. Rape can only be proven if the rapist confesses or if there are four male witnesses. A woman who alleges rape without the benefit of the act having been witnessed by four men, who support her claim, is actually confessing to having illicit sex. If she or the accused happens to be married, then the rape is considered to be adultery, and she is guilty according to the law. If the rapist claims that the act was consensual sex, there is very little that the woman can do to refute this. Islam places the burden of avoiding sexual encounters of any sort on the woman. The woman is accused and punished, and the man goes unpunished or is perhaps flogged.

One example of the tragic results of such law can be seen in the movie titled "The Stoning of M. Soraya." This movie, adapted from the novel *La Femme Lapide*, is based on the true story of a woman named Soraya living in the remote Iranian village of Kahpayeh. Her story is told by her Aunt Zahra. Soraya's abusive husband, Ali, tries to convince Soraya to grant him a divorce so that he can marry a girl who is only fourteen years old. Zahra, her Aunt, is talked into persuading Soraya to work for a widower by the village Mullah and the village mayor. As Soraya will be paid, she agrees to start working for him. Ali plans to use the unusual circumstance of her employment to spread lies that Soraya is being unfaithful to him so that she will be stoned and he can remarry. Ali and the Mullah start rumours about her infidelity so they can charge her with adultery. Ali and the Mullah need one more witness to Soraya's infidelity to be able to formally charge her. They visit the widower's house where she has been working and threaten the widower until he agrees to falsely accuse her and back up their accusations. Ali drags Soraya through the streets, beating her and publicly declaring that she has been unfaithful. When the widower lies and declares that they engaged in adultery, a trial is pursued. The conviction is upheld, and they prepare for the stoning of Soraya. She is buried in the ground up to her shoulders and then stoned to death by her family and other villagers.

Soraya's story is deeply shocking to those living in the West, yet I understand the restrictions and burden of Sharia only too well. I have lived surrounded by it—I have felt it, seen it, and breathed it.

Muslims claim that women have equal rights in Islam. Yet, if this is so, how are the many restrictions placed on women explained? If a Muslim woman has equal rights, then why is she not allowed to divorce her husband, while the man has complete freedom to do so? Why is the woman's position as a witness considered to be only fifty percent accurate, while the Muslim man's is one hundred percent? More importantly, a Muslim man will be granted the privilege of entering Paradise, yet ninety-nine percent of women, according to their prophet, will endure Hell.

Some women have claimed that they have converted to Islam because they were drawn to it while studying Islamic studies in college. Many have simply embraced it because they have met charming Muslim college students. Yet, in following Islam, they are signing up, not just to a religion, but to a lifestyle. Islam tells you how to dress, eat, pray, in which direction to pray, when to pray, who to talk to, and who not to talk to. Islam controls the whole of one's life, and if not followed exactly, one will not be allowed to enter into Paradise. Many, however, know the truth about Islam and want to leave it. Mosab Hassan Yousaf, son of an influential leader of the militant Hamas organization in the West Bank, is now a Christian. During a courageous interview, he said:

> "There are two facts that Muslims don't understand...First, I'd say about 95 percent of Muslims don't understand their own religion. It comes with a much stronger language than the language they speak, so they don't understand it. They rely only on religious people to get their knowledge about this religion. Second, they don't understand anything about other religions. Christian communities live between Muslims, and they are a minority. They (would) rather not speak out and tell people about Jesus because it's dangerous for them. So, all their ideas about other religions on earth are from Islamic perspectives. These two realities, most people don't understand. If people, if Muslims, start to understand religion—first of all, their religion—and see how awful stuff is in there, they'll start to figure out, this can't (be)... because most religious people focus on certain points of Islam. They have many points that they are very embarrassed to talk about."[1]

As you browse the first chapter of this book, you will begin to piece together the destructive way this religion influences male/female relationships in Middle Eastern and Asian countries, and even here in Europe and North America. Islamic culture has brought oppression, many times brutally, to Muslim women, and will continue to do so unless someone takes the bold step to draw aside its veil.

End Notes

1) www.foxnews.com/story/0,2933,402483.00.

Chapter 1
Brood of Vipers

May 22, 1981 is a day that I will remember for the rest of my life. My family and I were sitting on the veranda as the sun was beginning to set, discussing our plans for our upcoming vacation. Summer had always been an exciting time of the year, places to see and family members to visit. Dad and Mom were sipping hot English tea served with native finger food. I could see a dainty smile form as my mom looked into my dad's eyes, perhaps delighting at the sight of their three excited daughters.

This peaceful family moment did not last long. A man dressed in our native style approached my mother. While greeting her with, "Salam Madam Ji, Salam Saab," he handed her a piece of paper. He was offered a cup of tea, but he refused explaining that he had to run some errands and had only come to deliver the note.

After he left, my mom opened the note; I could see that gradually her expression changed. Her smile changed to a frown as her eyes filled with tears. She quietly got up and went inside as my dad followed. We could hear my parents discussing something; however, we could not figure out what was wrong. My mom's tears seemed to imply that something had gone seriously wrong.

When they came back to the veranda, my dad seemed sad, too. Mom had changed into her uniform, which was not unusual. Mom often went back to work at any hour of the day, since she was a nurse/teacher and matron of the nursing school. She was always on call, ready to tackle any emergency in the wards. However, this time, there was something different in the air. As my sisters and I questioned Dad, he said that Mom had to deal with a very important situation at the nursing school. He said that he was going to go with her; our aunt would babysit us. We were asleep by the time my parents returned that night.

The following day we awoke to find my parents already gone. I knew that Mom did not have to work, but that she and Dad had again returned to the school. My older sister and I were anxious to figure out this mystery that our parents were unwilling to tell us about. We told our aunt that we were going to our friend's house in the neighbourhood and would stay there until lunch (not quite the truth). We had plans to head to the nursing school without telling anyone.

The hospital where my mom worked was not a small hospital; it was a huge area where you would have to walk at least a mile before reaching a ward. We lived close to the nursing school, so we did not have to walk far. The streets were quiet, perhaps because of the unforgiving hot sun. In the distance, we could see groups of young female students in white uniforms walking swiftly toward the school. As we drew nearer, we heard faint sounds of mourning and crying. My heart started to beat faster, with the fear of finding something scary and, of course, mostly of being caught by our parents. The metal gate was unlocked. We pushed it slightly open and peeked inside very carefully to avoid being caught.

No one was around; we assumed that perhaps the gatekeeper had gone on a break. The wailing grew louder as we moved toward the building. In the middle of the courtyard, we saw a huge crowd of college girls, talking in low tones and sobbing. We had to get closer, but how could we push our way through such a large mob?

My sister pointed toward the upper floor where we could go to have a better look. From there, we saw what looked like a body in the courtyard partially covered with a white cotton sheet. I knew that face! It was Umber, a third-year nursing student, who often came to our house. Bewildered questions were running through my mind. It was the first time I had come face to face with death, and the shock was terrible.

"Let's go; I am frightened," my sister said. Thankfully, no one noticed us as we ran home as fast as we could. We had managed to calm down sufficiently by the time my parents returned in hope that our parents would not guess what we had been up to.

But that evening Mom asked, "Ok, what were you doing at the school?" Mom knew that she needed to share what had happened with us. She knew that this tragedy was a warning, which would help us to make the right decisions later in our life, especially when it was our time for marriage.

Mom told us that Umber had been a hard-working student when she initially came from a village. Brought up in a Christian family, she often ministered to her Christian classmates, regularly attending church services and holding prayer meetings. During her second year of college, she had started drifting away from her faith, gradually missing classes and failing to perform her nursing duties. Mom was beginning to worry about Umber, and her concern led her to investigate what was going on in the young student's life. To Mom's surprise, she discovered that Umber had fallen in love with a Muslim doctor and was secretly dating him.

In the Muslim world, having a boyfriend is a very foreign concept. It is taboo to choose your own husband or indulge in pre-marital sex. If a woman is found guilty of such behaviour, the level of punishment can vary. Among nominal Christians, who also do not allow choice in marriage, a woman may be disowned by family members or shunned by the community. Among Muslims, there is a great chance that overnight her parents will force her to marry someone of their choice. If the parents are very protective of their honor and follow the Islamic code of life strictly, then chances are they will kill their daughter, perhaps by stoning, hanging, strangling, or even slitting her throat.

When my mother found out about Umber, she tried to advise her. "Umber, remember you are bought by the Blood of Christ. Giving yourself to a non-believer would mean that you are rejecting Christ. There are so many Christian men working with you. Do you think you could consider the possibility of marrying one of them? Please, if you want to marry a man of your own choice, let it be a Christian. You do not know what will happen to you if you get married to this man. We are considered infidels, and unless you accept Islam, this man's family will never accept you."

But Umber's eyes, ears, and heart were closed to my mother's words. It is true that love makes one blind! Instead of listening to what my mother had to say, she turned on her. Later my mother brought this concern to her parents' attention, but somehow Satan had closed their minds as well. They thought that my mom was unnecessarily blaming their daughter and insulted her with abusive language. Mom was truly disheartened at Umber's reaction, for she did not want anyone disavowing Christ.

Umber truly believed that this man was in love with her. He would often buy her expensive gifts, but Mom never gave up on Umber and unceasingly prayed for her. Unfortunately, things became worse instead of better. For Mom, Umber's death was very painful. The autopsy report showed that Umber had probably committed suicide, as there were traces of rat poison in her blood. Many of her classmates did not believe the story, since they knew that Umber was not the type who would take her own life.

Several months after Umber's death, one of her colleagues named Gloria was on duty in the same ward where Umber's boyfriend was present. She overhead the doctor laughing with other male friends, telling them how Umber had screamed and pleaded for her life while she was being gang-raped. Gloria ran to the nursing school to inform the directors and the authorities, as well as all the teachers. The doctor was arrested and confessed that he and nine other colleagues planned to invite Umber to their dorm room. Umber thought that she was meeting Asad, her lover. However, Asad had invited his friends to enjoy her sexually because she was an infidel, and the Qur'an teaches that you can rape a non-Muslim woman. When Umber threatened to inform the police, the men plotted to kill her with the rat poison.

Asad was arrested along with the other nine men, but

soon the charges were dropped. The doctor claimed that Umber had seduced him on several occasions. Things had gotten out of control, and he had no choice. In Islam, a Muslim man is one hundred percent believable. His explanation was acknowledged, and all the men were released from jail. Dear Umber was now dead and buried in disgrace at the age of twenty-one. What a waste of a precious life! My Mom strongly believes that the Lord has brought her into her field of work so as to minister to young Christian girls and boys. Often the young girls are under the spell of charming Muslim men and are swiftly devoured as if by quicksand. Many lives have been changed by God's grace; however, many have been lost.

This is one story out of thousands. Many young girls have been and are suffering at the hands of what I call a "brood of vipers." Many of these girls are kidnapped, beaten, raped, and treated like slaves, perhaps becoming one of many wives. Within the Muslim world, almost all women are considered as sex objects and child-bearing machines. Why do these Muslim men treat the women in such a way? Is it the person himself who does this, or is he driven by his beliefs—and if so, what are they? The answer is simple: Muslim men are driven by an ideology or philosophy that dictates their way of thinking and acting.

This ideology is the outcome of the book called Qur'an, which is believed by every Muslim to be the verbatim word of Allah, whom they believe is god, as it was revealed to their prophet Muhammad, who is the founder of the Islamic religion and is believed to be the messenger of Allah by all Muslims. His words and sayings form the rule of life for all Muslims and his teachings on women and marriage drive the attitudes of Muslims everywhere. It is the teachings found in the Qur'an that lead to the low status of women in Muslim society.

But let us not forget that this ideology is seeping into the West, as well, as many more Muslims come to live in western countries and many westerners convert to Islam.

MARRIAGE:
A Serious Commitment

Marriage is a serious commitment that should be shared beautifully and sacrificially with someone. Whether the marriage succeeds or not will often depend on the choice a person makes as to whom to marry. The Western woman needs to understand that when she has a romantic encounter with a Muslim man who is charming to her, he could have ulterior motives. Is he truly in love with her, or does he have an agenda? What does his religion tell him to do? What does the Bible teach us about marrying a non-Christian? We need to go directly to the two sources—the Qur'an and the Bible—to the find the answers to these important questions.

The Qur'an

Islam has set down certain rules for Muslims when marrying a non-believer—or, as a Muslim would say, an infidel. It is clearly written in numerous verses that Allah hates Christians and Jews because of their beliefs. In fact, the Qur'an plainly commands Muslim believers not to even take unbelievers as friends. We can read this verse, for example:

"O you who believe! Do not take for intimate friends from among others than your own people, they do not fall short of inflicting loss upon you; they love what distresses you; vehement hatred has already appeared from out of their mouths, and what their breasts conceal is greater still; indeed. We have made the communications clear to you, if you will understand." Qur'an 3:118

There are other verses that also warn Muslims from associating or befriending non-Muslims, such as:

"O' you who believe! Do not take the Jews and Christians for friends; they are friends of each other; and whoever amongst you takes them for a friend then surely he is one of them; surely Allah does not guide the unjust people." Sura (or chapter) 5:51-52

The same tale goes even further condemning Muslims who do become friends with non-Muslims:

"You will see many of them befriending those who disbelieve; certainly evil is that which their souls have sent before for them, that Allah became displeased with them and in chastisement shall they abide." Sura 5:80

In view of such verses in the Qur'an, Muslims feel fear and distrust of non-Muslims and tend not to make close friendships with those outside their faith.

The Hadiths

Muslims also look to special books called the Hadiths to guide them in their lives and behavior. These are collections of the sayings of Muhammad, and many of them deal with whether a true Muslim can make friends with an infidel. One of Muhammad's sayings warns Muslims to consider carefully whom they choose as friends:

> "The prophet (peace-be-upon-him) said, 'A man follows the religion of his friend; so each one should consider whom he makes his friend.'"

And another clearly prohibits such friendship:

> "O you who believe! Take not my enemies and your enemies as friends offering them (your) love even they have disbelieved in that Truth (i.e., Allah, Prophet Muhammad, and this Quran) which has come to you."[1]

The Qur'an and the Hadiths have much to say about marriage between Muslims and non-Muslims. They teach that a Muslim woman must not marry a non-Muslim man. This stems from the view firmly taught in Islam that a man is the supreme authority and head of the family; thus, any Muslim woman who marries a non-believer will be under his authority and must follow his religion. Any children of their marriage will also be under his authority and will be obliged to follow their father's religion. Islam is patriarchal: a non-Muslim man will be seen to have full control in the marriage and family; a Muslim wife will always be answerable to her husband and under his authority. For this reason, Islam cannot allow

Muslim girls to marry outside of Islam, as they would be lost to the faith and would weaken the goal of Islam to become the world religion. The rules and prohibitions that are taught in Islam establish boundaries that make it impossible for a Muslim woman to enter into an inter-faith marriage.

One Muslim commentator, Yusuf Ali, warns against marrying those who do not follow Islam as follows:

> "Do not marry unbelieving women (idolaters), until they believe; a slave woman who believes is better than an unbelieving woman, even though she allures you. Nor marry (your girls) to unbelievers until they believe; a man slave who believes is better than an unbeliever, even though he allures you. Unbelievers do (but) beckon you to the Fire. But God beckons by His Grace to the Garden (of bliss) and forgiveness, and makes His Signs clear to mankind: That they may celebrate His praise." Yusuf Ali, Sura 2:221

The effects of this teaching can be seen in an experience I had four years ago. My close friend invited me to a bead party held at her home. Excitement and conversations floated around her living room, as the women got to know each other and chatted happily. Then I came across her, a Minister's wife who was hastily finishing her project to run back home and prepare to travel to Michigan to meet her son who had recently been married. She was so excited to share with us about the wedding of her son, and everyone's attention was drawn towards her. It all began when he met a Muslim girl from Pakistan in his college, dated for a while, and then had a grand wedding with all the Islamic ceremonies.

Her excitement about how the girl's family treated them with respect and honor was just flowing out of her. This lady's last sentence swept the ground from below my feet. She proudly announced that her son is now a convert to Islam. He even gave the Qur'an as a gift to his parents, and they were all very excited to read it and to know more about it. They felt that it should be honored as much as the Bible.

What is wrong with that picture? Well, almost everything. First of all, the above verse has come true. The young woman could not marry the woman's son until he believed, so he had to convert before the girl and his family would accept him. Now this young man believes that Allah is his god and Muhammad is his prophet. That means he has already denounced Christ and compromised on the deity of Christ. His conversion has caused a ripple effect; he will be attracting them (his parents and other relatives) with those ideas which they want to hear. It is impossible to convert to Islam without denying that Jesus is truly God, and this young man's conversion can only weaken the faith of his family as they seek to embrace Islam at the same time as Christianity. As Jesus said: "No-one can serve two masters, for either he will hate the one and love the other, or he will be devoted to the one and despise the other" Matthew 6:24.

THE MUSLIM MAN AND THE NON-MUSLIM WOMAN

In the case of a Muslim man wishing to marry a non-Muslim woman, the situation is not as definite as it would be for a Muslim girl marrying an infidel. Any non-Muslim male would have to accept Islam if he wished to marry a

Muslim girl, as Yusaf Ali's comments show. So marrying a non-Muslim woman still creates problems for a Muslim man unless she changes her faith or adopts the Muslim faith and becomes a "believer."

Although these verses strongly discourage a Muslim man from marrying a non-Muslim, under certain conditions, he can do so, especially if the marriage occurs in a non-Muslim country where Islamic law and religion do not prevail. What is the rationale behind this? Verse 2:221 of the Qur'an explicitly forbids Muslims from marrying unbelievers, even though Verse 5:5 allows it. It is interesting that Allah's change of mind corresponded somewhat curiously with Muhammad's own desire to marry a non-Muslim woman. One incident in Muhammad's life records that Muhammad went from one Jewish fort to another slaughtering the men and taking their wealth and women. He tortured to death the youthful Kiana and took his seventeen-year-old wife Safiya to a tent to have sex with her. His companions wondered whether she was Muhammad's captive or wife.[2]

Yusaf Ali reconciles the contradiction by saying that non-Muslim wives are "expected" to become Muslim. In Islam, the wife is under very heavy pressure to become Muslim, as the Qur'an shows. Even if the woman was not a Muslim before marriage, she can be a lawful wife if she converts to Islam, Qur'an 4:24.

> "(Lawful unto you in marriage) are (not only) chaste women who are believers, but chaste women among the People of the Book revealed before your time, when you give them their due dowries, and desire chastity, not lewdness, nor

secret intrigues. If anyone rejects faith, fruitless is his work, and in the Hereafter he will be in the ranks of those who have lost (all spiritual good)."
Yusuf Ali, Sura 5:5

Today billions of Muslims around the world consider non-Muslims as infidels. If we were still living in the seventh century, we who are not Muslim would be considered no less than a war prize. During my life living in my country, I witnessed countless numbers of non-Muslim girls marrying Muslim men. What happens to them after marriage and how they are treated by their husbands and in-laws is beyond the imagination of most women in the West. Though many wish to escape their bondage, it becomes virtually impossible for them.

One of my colleagues, Farah, confided in me that she wanted to leave her husband, as he was very abusive. There were days when she would take me to the staff room and show me bruises on her legs and back. Most of them were caused by a hose pipe.

One day, I took courage and asked her, "Farah, why don't you complain about him to your parents or friends?"

Her reply was that this could worsen her situation, as they would first blame her and, if they confronted him, he might become more aggressive and in anger possibly kill her. She was also concerned that her husband might take her son away from her. One particular day, she came to work all black and blue. This alerted all the staff members, but none dared to ask her about it. I approached her and asked Farah what had happened. First she denied anything had happened, and then she told me that her husband had beaten her merely because she had put a lot of spices in the food.

I said, "Farah, you need to do something about this. Just take your son and run away."

She looked straight in my eyes and said, "You have no idea, have you? Don't you understand he will come after me and kill me? I have nowhere to go and nowhere to hide. This is my fate, and I have to endure it." She soon resigned and never got in touch with anyone. I still remember her pretty face with a very saddened heart.

You perhaps also remember in 2010 *Time* magazine published a front page picture of an eighteen-year-old Afghan girl, who tried to escape her abusive husband and in-laws. Unfortunately she was caught, and on the orders of a Taliban judge, her husband sliced her ears and then her nose, in order to deter other girls in the village from running away from their husbands. This was her punishment for escaping from her horrible marriage.

End Notes

1) Sahih Bukhari 50:572

2) Qur'an 4:24

Chapter 2
Love is Blind, but Marriage is an Eyeopener

HAZEL AND UMAR

Let me share another incident that took place here in the United States when Hazel, an American, met and fell in love with Umar, a Pakistani Muslim student. He was a very handsome, charming college student who dated Hazel for six months. Hazel was deeply impressed with his westernized and liberal ideas. To her, he was a true gentleman who loved her dearly. During their courtship, Umar painted a beguiling picture of his home, his family, and his friends back in Pakistan, as well as his family's status in their community.

Hazel and Umar were married after only a few months and began what was an exciting life for the young couple— or so thought Hazel. During this time, Umar began working on changing his status in the U.S. from student to citizen. They eventually discovered that Hazel was pregnant, bringing joy to both of them.

Hazel gave birth to a baby girl, whom Umar named Fatima. But the honeymoon period was now over, as Hazel began to see changes in Umar's behavior. He began praying five times a day, which he had never done before. He asked his wife to wear a hijab (head covering), and he objected to Hazel going out in public wearing what he called "inappropriate clothes," such as jeans, t-shirts, or a two-piece bathing suit. Hazel was quite surprised at Umar's change in attitude and chose to ignore it. Umar stopped helping around the house, and petty quarrels began arising, causing tensions between the two of them.

When Fatima was a year old, Umar announced that he wanted to visit his family in Pakistan. He convinced Hazel that the visit to her in-laws would provide a welcome change for the young family.

When they arrived in Pakistan, Hazel was treated like a celebrity. However, her "high" status existed only within the circle of a few women and within the four walls of her in-laws' home. She was not allowed to enter any room where other men were present, including a room where Umar met with his friends and other male relatives. Hazel realized that this restricted life applied not just to her but to all the women of the family.

Additional restrictions on Hazel's movements grew as the weeks went by. One morning, Umar's mother brought the Qur'an into her room and asked Hazel to join all of the ladies in prayer. Hazel's uneasiness grew as she refused to participate in the gathering. Seeing his wife's refusal and what he saw as a refusal to obey, Umar beat her and told her to recite their Kalma (creed): "(There is) none worthy of worship except Allah. Muhammad is Messenger of ALLAH." This creed is recited when anyone converts to Islam.

Refusing to recite the creed, Hazel realized that their marriage was in trouble. Hazel had already decided to return to their home in the United States. Sharing her decision with Umar, he took her by surprise when he agreed. However, he had already amended his plans to continue his stay in Pakistan. Hazel had misunderstood Umar's kind gesture in allowing her to leave. Sadly, it became clear to Hazel that she could not bring her daughter with her back to the United States. He was allowing her to go, but not with their daughter Fatima.

After returning home, Hazel did everything in her power through legal action to get her daughter back, but unfortunately, she could not. Hazel has since then accepted Christ into her life and now works as a church secretary. Jesus has healed all of her wounds and suffering. She has remarried a Christian and has two children in her new family, but she can never forget the sorrow of losing her daughter. We met Hazel and her family in one of the church meetings. As she spoke, tears poured down her face, and I could feel her pain. She expressed to me that the day she sat on the aircraft, she was in excruciating pain. It was a pain that could not be described, only felt. She still wonders if she will ever be allowed to see her daughter. She is grateful for God's grace, which gave her strength without which she would have not survived her tragedy. She has courageously allowed us to share her sad story of her marriage to a Muslim man.

JADE AND DAWOOD (DAVID)

Jade was working as a member of a mission team in a church that evangelizes among the Muslims. She believed that she could bring about change and was challenged that she would be able to convert at least one person in a year.

During this period, she met Dawood, a young Iraqi Muslim, while distributing Bibles in a predominantly Muslim neighborhood. Jade found it interesting that Dawood was always willing to hear what she was sharing and seemed open to the news that she was bringing about Christ. He would often invite her for coffee and would discuss some of his questions about the Bible. Jade felt that she was clearly making a difference in Dawood's life. Gradually, she began getting closer to him, and their causal relationship turned into friendship and then to love. Contrary to her beliefs, Jade engaged in a sexual relationship, as well.

Dawood told Jade that he belonged to a very wealthy family back in Iraq and had come to the United States in an effort to increase his wealth. The church, however, had no idea as to what Dawood's motives were. Jade thought that her love would win his heart, that he would start going to church with her, and that he would finally accept Christ into his life. Within eight months after meeting, Dawood proposed to her. Jade was overjoyed at the thought of marriage to him.

Dawood had already decided that the wedding ceremony would take place in Iraq, with a second ceremony in the United States after their return. The excitement of everything associated with the frantic wedding plans obscured the trap that was being set by Dawood.

Jade and Dawood were married in Iraq, but things did not work out quite the way Jade had planned. Because she loved him so much and did not want to part with him, she converted to Islam rather than him converting to Christianity. Sadly, she embraced Islam and now lives as Aisha rather than by her American name, Jade. She is ashamed to return to the United States to tell her side of the story. We learned of her story from her mother, who was very hurt and constantly weeps for her lost daughter. Instead of Jade/Aisha gaining a soul for Christ, she lost hers to Islam.

The question arises from this sad story: was Jade well-rooted in her Christian beliefs? Was she well-acquainted with Islam and its dangers? Did she even delve into the Qur'an before taking the challenge with her new husband?

Let's examine what the Bible says about our relationships with non-believers. The Scriptures clearly declare:

> "Be ye not unequally yoked together with unbelievers: for what fellowship hath righteousness with unrighteousness? and what communion hath light with darkness?" 2 Corinthians 6:14

While this passage does not specifically mention marriage, it definitely has implications for marriage. The passage continues, "What harmony is there between Christ and Belial? What does a believer have in common with an unbeliever…?"

Even though this verse does not directly refer to interfaith marriage, the apostle Paul is not encouraging the Corinthians to isolate themselves from unbelievers but is discouraging the compromise with their sinful values and practices that marrying an unbeliever will involve them in.

In 1 Corinthians 15:33, Paul tells his readers:

> "Be not deceived: evil communications corrupt good manners."

Having any kind of an intimate relationship with an unbeliever can quickly and easily turn into something that hinders your walk with Christ. We are called to evangelize the lost, not to be intimate with them. There is nothing wrong with building friendships with unbelievers, but that is as far as it should go. If you are dating an unbeliever, what should be your priority: romancing him or winning his soul for Christ? If you marry an unbeliever, how would the two of you cultivate spiritual intimacy in your marriage? How could a quality marriage be built if you disagree on the most crucial aspect—belief in Jesus Christ?

I met Pastor Soto in Canada six months ago. Because of possible danger to him, I cannot reveal any details about him. During his time in serving the Lord, he met many young Canadian women who were dating Muslim men and wanted to get married, but were not sure whether they were making the right decision or not. Pastor Soto wrote an article titled "Must I marry a believer?" which he gladly shared with me. I wish to share his insights with you, as well:

> "Marriage is a union meant to resemble and represent the love between Jesus Christ and His church. This love is both birthed and sustained by and within the nature of Christ. Marriage to God is more than mere loyalty and fidelity, but rather it is a matter of identity. We become one with Christ whilst simultaneously becoming one with our spouse, and so to mix ourselves with a non-believer is to defile the temple of the Holy Spirit and mix Jesus with a non-believer. The Christian marriage is one of appropriated headship and co-submis-

sion. The Christian view of marriage holds both man and woman as equal in identity whilst separate in expression (gender role), but what keeps a Christian marriage balanced is that the identity of the couple as a union and as individuals is rooted in who Jesus said we are."

The New Testament states that the soon-to-be married couple should be on equal footing. In 1 Corinthians 7:39, it states that a Christian woman may marry a Christian man and vice versa. Paul writes further,

"Be ye not unequally yoked together with unbelievers: for what fellowship hath righteousness with unrighteousness? and what communion hath light with darkness? And what concord hath Christ with Belial? or what part hath he that believeth with an infidel? And what agreement hath the temple of God with idols? for ye are the temple of the living God; as God hath said, I will dwell in them, and walk in them; and I will be their God, and they shall be my people. Wherefore come out from among them, and be ye separate, saith the Lord, and touch not the unclean thing; and I will receive you." 2 Corinthians 6:14-18

At first glance, this divine counsel seems too restrictive, but when viewed more closely, it demonstrates a great deal of wisdom. If a married couple starts life in the same faith and theology, then this removes the pressure of possibly converting the partner to the other's faith. One partner is not evangelizing the other.

In Biblical Christianity, the man and the woman have a deep, spiritual relationship with Jesus Christ even before they become one flesh in marriage. Therefore, their spiritual intimacy with the Lord will be shared within the couple's intimacy in the marriage. This true equality discourages patriarchy in a marriage: the wife already agrees with the husband in religious matters, so what needs does he have to control the relationship and set forth religious laws?[1]

It is important to understand that Islam has a completely different theology. In one crucial aspect, we can see how marriage between a Christian and a Muslim creates an unbridgeable gulf between them. Muhammad denied the "Sonship" of Christ and instead demoted Him to the status of a prophet. But for a Christian believer, the fact that Jesus Christ is the Son of God, truly God and truly man, is an essential and non-negotiable teaching in Christianity. We must not compromise the deity of Christ, no matter what situation we find ourselves in.

THE AFTERMATH OF MARRIAGE TO A MUSLIM

The Internet gives us free access to many good as well as bad things. Although many young girls have probably read on the Internet and in other places what the ideology of Islam can do in their lives, they are still willing to jump into this pool of quicksand. They mistakenly believe that other women who are suffering have brought this punishment on themselves. These young girls think that love can conquer all. They do not completely understand the different beliefs of Christianity and Islam. They do not realize that if a young girl marries a Muslim man, she will have to give up her faith and convert to Islam. Even after reading true stories and accounts of difficulties women and girls have encountered, these girls still consent to marry a Muslim. Why does this happen? There are several reasons why a girl will find marriage with a Muslim attractive:

1. They are disillusioned with Christianity and the society they see around them. There seems to be a spiritual vacuum in their lives. They believe that perhaps a change in religion will fill this emptiness.

2. Some women convert to Islam simply because they believe that there is little difference between Christianity and Islam. Therefore, they feel it does not matter which they choose to follow. Their Muslim friends speak of Jesus, how He was born of a virgin, was sinless, and performed miracles. However, they talk of Christ as merely a prophet, NOT as the Son of God. For Muslims, it is blasphemy to proclaim that God has a son. But these young women are happy to hear that Muslims honor Jesus and do not realize what is missing from the conversation they have with their Muslim friends regarding Jesus.

3. One attraction of Islam is that the practices and beliefs are set out simply and are easy to understand and follow, such as when to pray, how to pray, what to eat, how to dress, and so on.

4. In some cases, a woman has been hurt emotionally earlier in her life by her parents, a boyfriend, or an ex-husband, and is now desperate to enter into a new relationship. Of course, she has no idea that

her new relationship with a Muslim man is only pretence on his part. Many young women come from dysfunctional families and enter into such a relationship when they themselves are emotionally unstable. They feel protected with the Muslim man and feel a sense of wholeness and happiness in the relationship. Of course, this does not last.

5. Some choose this avenue because of rebelliousness toward their parents. Forbidden love (particularly on the part of the Muslim man's family who will not allow him to marry a non-Muslim) creates a challenge for the young woman to entice him into a relationship.

6. When the woman is dating the Muslim man, she may be introduced to his family. Initially they make her feel very welcome. Western society believes in the freedom of the individual. In contrast, Muslim culture believes in a community system called UMMA. The family is close-knit and always there for each other during good times and bad. This is a great attraction for the young woman as she feels protected and secure within the family structure.[2]

Why would a Muslim man consent to marry a Western or infidel woman? We need to understand the thought process of a Muslim man, where he comes from, what he thinks of western society, and above all, what his ideology teaches him. Sadly, the Muslim man does not have a high opinion of women in general. A woman's worth is tied to her child-bearing abilities. It is even worse when it concerns a western woman (labeled an 'infidel' in Islam). Thanks to the spread of Hollywood's culture and immorality, the respect for western women has diminished in the eyes of men living in the Muslim world. The media present a very low image of western society in the opinion of Muslims generally, especially those who have never been to the West. Most Muslims believe that all Westerners behave in the way that is depicted in the movies they see. In the Muslim's mind, everyone falls into that category. Then the question arises: why then are Muslim men interested in marrying western women?

Simply put, a western woman becomes a medallion because of her race. Muslims reject western culture and its form of democracy. They follow the Islamic law (Sharia), but they love the prosperity and freedom that the western nations offer. For the Muslim man, marriage to a Westerner means a great deal. Some of these women are targeted for the sole purpose of obtaining a visa. The Muslim will pretend to be committed to the marriage until he receives a permanent visa, and then things change. By this time, he is able to work, earn good money, and support a family back home. He is then in a position to sponsor his original family so they can enjoy prosperity in the West.

Muslim men from wealthy families, however, often have a different motive, which has more repercussions for the West and does not augur well for a happy marriage. In Islam, it is permissible for a Muslim man to marry a Christian or Jewish woman, but not the other way around. Such marriages are encouraged as they are a legitimate means of "dawah," which means Muslim evangelism or mission, a way of spreading of Islam. When a wealthy Muslim man courts a young western girl, he appears to be very romantic, passionate, and intelligent. During this courting phase, he talks of Christ as if he knew Him personally; then he smoothly attempts to integrate Islam with Christianity, pointing out some of the apparent commonalities of both religions and presenting Islam as peaceful. This is part of his missionary strategy to present Islam in a very appealing way.[3]

But changes come about after such a marriage. Whenever two people from different cultures unite, they face major cultural challenges. What happens to a non-Muslim woman who steps into an inter-faith marriage with a Muslim man?

The family plays a vital role in the household in all countries where Islam holds sway. The family, despite minor misunderstandings, is tightly-knit, and family members are very dependent upon one another. When the man brings his foreign wife home to his family, he undergoes a transformation of character. He is no longer "the lord of the land" but is now subject to his father and mother. A Muslim man is also supposed to listen and obey his parents, since the parents are the final authority over how the household is run. This power of authority will greatly influence, if not control, the non-Muslim bride's life. If she is rebellious in her acceptance of Islamic culture, her situation will worsen. If she questions her husband, she will soon discover that he is following the Islamic system and will not compromise for his new wife. Pressure increases on the new wife, as the man's family may encourage him to take a second wife of their choosing. The devastating result is that the western wife is not ready for the fact that any matrimonial problems in the Muslim marriage are always decided in favor of Islamic law.

Since the man has many friends, he will be honored among them not only because he has successfully married a western woman, but also because he has been able to convert her. Even though he is very proud to have won this trophy, he will never show her to his friends unless she is appropriately dressed. Many western customs are not acceptable in the eyes of a Muslim. In the West, couples may dance together, as well as joke and kiss one another in public as a sign of friendship. This is totally prohibited in Islam. Men and women are isolated in social settings, with the men in one room and the women in another. The Muslim's wife will never be allowed to have a member of the opposite sex as a friend, and it is absolutely prohibited for her to speak to a man outside of the family unit.

Should the Muslim husband bring his wife and children to his homeland, Islamic society is mostly responsible for the teaching of Islam. From the beginning, the children will learn about Islam in bits and pieces at home and school, via the radio and television, and even through participation in classes with Islamic students and political parties. The grandparents, aunts, and uncles will also help teach Islamic values to the children.

Should the Muslim family reside in the West, the situation is different. In most cases, the parents are probably the only bridge between Islam and the children. The husband will try to implement Islamic law in the household. He will try to live close to members of the Muslim community, giving his children an opportunity to mingle with other Muslim children. He will enforce Halal (food which is lawful as defined by Allah the almighty) and discourage alcoholic beverages in the house. Daughters will be discouraged from wearing western garments that expose too much of their bodies.

Many women who marry Muslim men are shocked to see a sudden transformation in their husbands. The attentive boyfriend, now her husband, has turned into a complete stranger. He is now very reserved and shows no display of affection. In addition, he will not offer any assistance with the household chores, since he has been taught that running the house, parenting the children, and serving the guests is considered the woman's job. Any disobedience on her part could lead him to physically abuse his non-Muslim wife. It is very common for the man to beat his wife, as it is commanded in the Qur'an, Sura 4:34. This verse says that a man should admonish a wife if he sees her ill-conduct, and if she persists in this, he may refuse to share her bed and beat her. This practice is against the law in western countries and creates huge problems for women marrying into Islam.

Tina was another Christian woman I knew personally back in my country who lived a couple of houses away from ours. It was a small neighborhood. Everyone knew everyone, and any actions were hard to hide. She was found dating a Muslim man, who was her colleague. Though her parents warned her of the consequences of having a relationship with a Muslim, she turned a deaf ear to their advice. One day, she eloped with him and got married. It was not a big wedding; just her presence in the mosque and the recitation of Islamic creed was enough. Shakeel was the groom's name, and he was the oldest of the nine siblings. Tina conceived within the first months of her marriage. The day she delivered, her mother-in-law took the child into her own care immediately from the hospital and refused to allow him to be nursed by his mother. According to her, she did not want the milk of an infidel to run in the child's veins.

Recently, I was able to go back to my home country and got the opportunity to visit my old neighborhood. Many things had changed, and several of my neighbors had moved. Yet, one thing brought my memories back, and that was that I was able to meet Tina. She is the mother of six boys now, and I took courage to ask her how she had been. She did not have much to say, yet every word that she uttered implied an intense feeling of regret, fear, and emptiness.

I have known many women personally who married Muslim men and now live in regret. There are many more such stories I could tell, and the truth is that I am just scratching the tip of the iceberg. Tina's experience is typical of the heartache suffered by so many women who have left their Christian faith to marry into Islam.

End Notes

1) www.answering-Islam.org/author.../mixed_marriage

2) Rosemary Sookhdeo, Why Christian Women convert to Islam.

3) Ibid.

Chapter 3
Her First Veil

L et me take you on a journey down the path of a young Muslim girl and her submission to her god, Allah. Her life is orchestrated by the decisions made by the male members of her family. She is raised with the mindset that she is the weaker vessel and has no ability to make decisions on her own.

In Islam, a young girl is considered fit for marriage from the time she reaches puberty. At this point, she begins to cover herself with a veil (abaaya) in order to protect herself from the lustful eyes of men. The Muslim girl lives strictly within the confines of her home and may attend social gatherings only when accompanied by family members. She, along with other women in the family, must remain covered (especially the head and chest) when venturing out in public places. From the time a girl starts her menstrual cycle, she is greatly valued for her virginity and remains at the mercy of her eagle-eyed father, brothers, or grandfather to choose a husband for her. Often this decision will be based on possible personal or economic gain for the family through the union; there is no higher authority to whom she may go to question the decision.[1]

MY CHILDREN'S FATE

Historically, arranged marriages have been commonly practiced in Asia, but evidence suggests that arranged marriages were once a custom in the West. Ancient societies were regulated so as to nurture a system of inheritance. Laws were passed for property and land allocation. In some cases, a marriage would be arranged to avoid a bloody battle.[2]

It is rare to find an arranged marriage now within western cultures. However, it still remains a part of eastern cultures. In Muslim nations, pre-marital dating is considered taboo. Most of the time, a young couple does not have the opportunity to see each other before the wedding day. They will have to start their life together, including their love life, on the day of their wedding. The two will have had no courtship; perhaps they will fall in love, perhaps not. An arranged marriage is really a union of both families.

While I was working in an educational institution, my colleague Nargis asked me to bring in my wedding video. She was excited to see a Christian marriage and was curious to know how it took place. She brought her wedding video in, too, and in our spare time, we sat in the library to compare notes. We saw hers first, and then it was time to watch mine. During the segment where my husband and I were exchanging our wedding vows, Nargis began to cry.

I asked her, "Nargis, why are you crying?" She confessed that she was so touched to see that we Christians were joyful as we professed our "I do's" in front of the entire congregation. At first, I did not understand why she became so emotional about this until she told me her true feelings. Nargis had been given in marriage to a man she had never seen before. The following story is how she recalled her wedding day.

"I was in my house miles away from where my husband-to-be was. I sat in my room unaware of the noises around me. My mom said that I was the most beautiful bride that anyone had ever seen. I wore a red dress and was adorned with gold jewelry. A thin curtain divided my room and the living room. All the women from my immediate family and my future in-laws were gathered in the living room. Loud chatter and laughter filled the house for hours, and then, all of a sudden, silence descended as if a storm was about to come.

"The women covered their heads and faces and started moving toward the other room. The men entered and settled in the living room. The Muslim clergyman (Mulana) accompanied my father, along with a few other men I did not recognize. The curtain was meant to obstruct my view into the other room, but it did not. I could hear my heart pounding. My mom was the only person with me, and she saw how nervous I was. My hands and feet started sweating as the Mulana began reciting the Islamic creed and reading from the Qur'an. Then he loudly asked me three times: 'Do you take Adnan bin Saleem (son of Saleem) as your husband?' Can you believe that all three times my mother replied 'YES' instead of me? Then I was handed a register to sign. The register was passed back to the Mulana to get signatures from the witnesses. Sounds of Mubarak Ho! Mubarak Ho! (Congratulations) broke out. The deed was done."

While Nargis was telling me her story, she was sobbing. At that point, I could not understand her pain, which seemed so deep, and I could not understand why her mom had said 'Yes' during the wedding ceremony instead of her.

She continued, "I had never seen Adnan in person or in a photograph. I did not know what I was about to get in my package. During my Nikkah (Arabic for matrimonial contract between a Muslim bride and groom), I was so tense that my words would not come out of my mouth. So my mother pretended to be me and said 'Yes.' When the papers were handed to me, my mom whispered in my ear, 'Please sign; this is a matter of your father's honor.'"

Nargis told me that she had never wanted to be married to a stranger, but she had no choice. She finished by telling me, "Can you imagine, I saw my husband for the first time when I was in bed with him!"

Nargis was twenty-five years old when she married, which is very rare in the Muslim world. She was one of the lucky women who belonged to an educated and wealthy family, and she was able to complete her studies before getting married. Not all are that lucky. Thousands of others (especially those girls born into poor families) are sold or given in marriage to strangers who are often old enough to be their grandfathers. Only a handful of girls are lucky enough to marry the man of their choice.

Although arranged marriages are often a cultural practice, it is strongly taught in Islam. Although the Qur'an and the Hadiths talk about requesting the woman's consent, this is often ignored in practice. A verse in the Qur'an says:

> "Do not prevent them (women) from marrying their husbands when they agree between themselves in a lawful manner."[3]

However, Imam Malik, one of the four great Imams of the Sunni schools of Islamic jurisprudences, explains this verse in a much stricter fashion than might be thought on first reading. He makes the choice of a partner by a Muslim girl subject to the over-ruling power or ijbar of her father or guardian in the interest of the girl herself.[4]

In one of the most authoritative books of the sayings of Muhammad, the following passages seems to allow for consent of young girls to being given in marriage.

Allah's apostle said,

> "A lady slave should not be given in marriage until she is consulted, and a virgin should not be given in marriage until her permission is granted." The people said, "How will she express her permission?" The Prophet said, "By keeping silent (when asked her consent)." Some people said, "If a man, by playing a trick, presents two false witnesses before the Judge to testify that he has married a matron with her consent and the Judge confirms his marriage, and the husband is sure that he has never married her (before), then such a marriage will be considered as a legal one, and he may live with her as husband."[5]

In another passage, Aisha, Muhammad's young wife, relates a conversation she had with him:

> I asked the Prophet, "O Allah's Apostle! Should the women be asked for their consent to their marriage?" He said, "Yes!" I said, "A virgin, if asked, feels shy and keeps quiet." He said, "Her silence means her consent." Bukhari: Book #85, Hadith #79.

What I want to focus on are Muhammad's words taken from these Hadiths that "her silence means her consent." What do you think is the actual meaning of this phrase? A young girl, who is a virgin living in a Muslim country, is taught over and over again throughout her life to protect the honor of her family. One wrong move can cause a disaster not only for her, but for her entire family. If a proposal comes for her, it will be the male members of the family who decide which man is best for her. If she is given the chance to speak and rejects the choice of her parents, she will be considered disrespectful and disobedient. So, in order to avoid been beaten or possibly killed, she maintains her silence. Therefore, knowing what the consequences could be, she will not take any decision.

Now place yourself in a young girl's shoes and imagine how you would feel if the most important decision of your life, your marriage, was made by someone other than you. Generally, in most Muslim areas, the family's opinion is still considerate for the young girl, and they show a photograph of the husband-to-be to her. However, since the daughter's silence is often misconstrued as her consent, she is handed over to a man she has never met and with whom she is expected to spend the rest of her life.

Millions of Muslims around the world decide their children's fate based on the teachings of Islam. Is that why they arrange for their children (especially girls, although boys may sometimes have arranged marriages also) to be married at a very young age? What is the basis for this? This practice of arranged marriages, even of very young girls, is attested in many Islamic books, especially the Hadiths and Imam Ghazali's book, Ihya Uloom Ed-Din, which is considered as sacred as the Qur'an.

It is this teaching that gives divine authority to these practices and is why Muslims throughout the world continue to uphold a custom, which is so very different from the way people in the West choose a marriage partner.

CHILD MARRIAGES

In the West, the idea of child marriage is shocking, and there are laws to protect young girls from being exploited in this way. In many Muslim countries, however, the situation is very different. Muhammad himself, who is considered the perfect man, married his youngest wife, Aisha, when she was only six years old. Her father, Abu Bakr, a good friend of Muhammad's, gave her hand in marriage to the much older prophet. Many Muslims claim that it was Abu Bakr who approached Muhammad asking him to marry his young daughter, but it is recorded in one of the Hadiths:

> "The Prophet asked Abu Bakr for Aisha's hand in marriage, but Abu Bakr said, 'But I am your Brother.' The Prophet said, 'You are my Brother in Allah's religion and His book, but she (Aisha) is lawful for me to marry.'" Sahih Bukhari 7:18

Abu Bakr and Muhammad had made a pledge to each other to be brothers, so that made Aisha Muhammad's niece. Yet that did not stop Muhammad from asking for her hand at such a tender age. Later she became his favorite wife, as she was so young, fresh, and untouched.[6]

History tells us that Muhammad consummated the marriage when Aisha turned nine years old. It seems as if there was no objection on her part; why would there be, as she was still playing with her dolls at that age. The Interpreter wrote (Aisha):

> "I used to play with the dolls in the presence of the Prophet, and my girlfriends also used to play with me. When Allah's Apostle used to enter (my dwelling place), they used to hide themselves, but the Prophet would call them to join and play with me." Sahih Bukhari, Vol. 8, Book 73 # 151

Playing with dolls and similar images is forbidden in Islam, but it was allowed for Aisha at that time, as she was a little girl who had not yet reached puberty.

Did Aisha know what was going to happen to her? Did her parents require her to give her consent? Muhammad teaches his followers to obtain the consent of their daughters regarding their upcoming marriages. Of course, we have seen in the Hadiths that silence means consent.

Several Hadiths suggests that Muhammad had sex with Aisha in her house when she was nine years old. Sahih Bukhari and Sunan of Abu Dawud record Aisha's own reminiscences when she said,

> "...that the Prophet wrote the marriage contract with her when she was six years old, and he consummated his marriage when she was nine years old. Hisham said, 'I have been informed that Aisha remained with the Prophet for nine years' (i.e., until his death)." Bukhari, Vol. 7 Book 62 # 88

Aisha continues expressing her heart when she says:

> The Apostle of Allah married me when I was
> seven years old. (The narrator said "or six
> years.") He had intercourse with me when I
> was nine years old." Hadiths of Sunan of Abu
> Dawud, volume 2, # 2116

All Aisha knew was that Muhammad was a special person, and her father adored him. Muslims believe that whatever he did was "culturally acceptable in that era." If we believe this story, then we can see why Muslims are still practicing today what was acceptable in Muhammad's time. Muhammad set an example and established cultural norms that continue into the 21st century. Thus, his followers still believe that it is not morally wrong or barbaric to take very young girls as their wives.

Do the parents of these young girls think that marrying off their young daughters is cruel or barbaric? Are the cries of these little girls heard? What are the consequences of these situations? Sadly, many young girls experience extreme depression, and some may even commit suicide. Child abuse is legal in the Islamic world today! Many children are forced by their fathers, their family, or because of family finances, to accept marriage with men who are old enough to be their grandfathers. Many do not understand what they are getting into when they or their families are approached.[7]

This is a part of Islam that Muslims living in the West will not tell you. When a Muslim is approached with questions querying whether Muhammad was right in marrying a young child, or whether it is lawful for you to give your daughters away in marriage at a very young age, you might hear different responses. First, a Muslim may act very defensively. You will hear hundreds of excuses to cover up the indecent acts of Muhammad. Second, there is a group of Muslims who will justify the action by saying that since it was culturally acceptable during Muhammad's era, it should be acceptable in the twenty-first century. Or you may hear nothing from some individuals who are probably ashamed, but will not openly condemn the act, simply because it would put their lives in danger. Aisha, the child-wife of Muhammad, is specially honored in Islam. She is known as the "Mother of Believers." Every Muslim knows her story, and many name their daughters after her.

MUSLIM SCHOLARS AND ILLOGICAL REASONING

Deception and intimidation are tools that Muslims use to defend their false teachings. When it comes to the issue of child marriage, this is no exception. Because of its many endorsements within Islamic scripture, child marriage is permitted by a majority of Muslim scholars and leaders. Here is just an example of what several have admitted:

Dr. Abd Al-Hamid Al_Ubeidi writes:

> "There is no minimum marriage age for either men or women in Islamic law. The law in many countries permits girls to marry only from the age of eighteen. This is arbitrary legislation, not Islamic law...In some Islamic countries, the age of maturity can be eight or ten years...Many criminals,

the enemies of Islam, ask: How could the Prophet Muhammad, at fifty-two years of age, marry Aisha when she was only six years, and consummate the marriage when she was nine years old? I say to them: People who live in glass houses shouldn't throw stones. Why do you permit your young girls to fornicate? They consider it one of their liberties. Therefore, in these Islamic countries, you rarely find girls age ten or twelve who are still virgins."[8]

Sheikh Hamoud Hashim al Tharibi also remarks:

"Because this happened to the Prophet, we cannot tell people that it is prohibited to marry at an early age...Our mothers and before them our grandmothers married when they were barely ready to perform all marital duties at that age."[9]

Sheikh Abdul Aziz Al Sheikh—Grand Mufti of Saudi Arabia—is of the same opinion, saying:

"It is incorrect to say that it's not permitted to marry off girls who are fifteen and younger. A girl aged ten or twelve can be married. Those who think she's too young are wrong, and they are being unfair to her. We hear a lot in the media about the marriage of underage girls. We should know that Sharia law has not brought injustice to women."[10]

Late Ayatollah Khomeini of Iran, Supreme Leader of Islamic Revolution, was particularly supportive of early marriage for young girls, giving a detailed judgment about it, writing:

> "A man can marry a girl younger than nine years of age, even if the girl is still a baby being breast-fed. A man, however, is prohibited from having intercourse with a girl younger than nine; other sexual acts, such as foreplay, rubbing, kissing, and sodomy are allowed. A man having intercourse with a girl younger than nine years of age has not committed a crime, but only an infraction if the girl is not permanently damaged. If the girl, however, is permanently damaged, this man must provide for her for all her life. But this girl will not count as one of the man's four permanent wives. He is also not permitted to marry the girl's sister."[11]

The following leading Muslims strongly support the teaching of Islam about the marriage of young girls.

Dr. Ahmad al-Mulbi, Saudi Marriage Officiate, said:

> "You can have a marriage contract with a one-year-old, not to mention a girl of seven, eight, or nine. But is the girl ready for sex or not? What is the appropriate age for sex for the first time? This varies according to environment and tradition."[12]

Imam Sani, a Nigerian Cleric, said:

> "Child marriage in Islam is permissible. In the Quran, there is no specific age of marriage."[13]

Sheikh Mohammad al Hazni, a Legislator in Yemen, said:

"Everything that is not forbidden is permitted. (The new law in Yemen that set the minimum marriage age at seventeen is a Western plot aimed at westernizing our culture. The West wants to teach us how to marry, conceive, and divorce. This is cultural colonization that we reject."[14]

These are some statements of just a few Muslim leaders and scholars expressing their views on the issue of child marriage. Many other Muslim scholars hold similar views. Therefore, do not be surprised when you read and hear about young Muslim daughters marrying old men. It is not their fault ... they are simply following their prophet.

THE DESTINY OF A CHILD BRIDE IN THE 21st CENTURY

The example set by Muhammad has brought nothing but agony to the innocent girls of the Muslim world. They are children, like ours, and have the desire to run and play and go to school. They probably would like to snuggle with their parents and be free of thoughts of cooking, cleaning, or doing laundry. All of their dreams are shattered when they are handed over to a man who is four, five, six, or even seven times older. They become no more than young servants for these older men with lustful eyes.

Does slavery exist today within Islamic society? The answer is yes. It has always been a part of Islamic society.

Sheikh Saleh Al-Fawzan, a member of the Senior Council of Clerics, Saudi Arabia's highest religious body, said:

> "Slavery is a part of Islam ...Slavery is part of jihad, and jihad remains as long there is Islam... [Those who argue that slavery has been abolished are] ignorant, not scholars. They are merely writers. Whoever says such things is an infidel."[15]

Slavery does exist in parts of the Islamic world today, and, of course, foreign workers in Saudi Arabia are often viewed as slaves. Muhammad does not condemn slavery; in fact, he owned many himself. In some ways, these young girls who are married off early are slaves. Shamefully, it is the parents themselves who believe their daughters are a burden on the family and need to be married off as soon as possible. The basic reason is the intention to preserve family honor by helping her avoid pre-marital sex. According to Muhammad, women have a deficiency of mind, and thus, it is assumed by Muslims that a woman has no ability to make correct decisions. She can easily get swayed and become involved in sexual relationships. So, in order to avoid shame, her parents get her married at a young age when she is dependent on their decision.

Sons, on the other hand, are preferred, as they are believed to carry on the family name and faith. Another reason for the preference for boys is Islamic inheritance laws, which give double to boys as they do to girls. It is expected that males in the family are to be financially responsible for women under their care.

The result of such young marriages is tragic in many cases. CNN reported that:

"A twelve-year-old Yemeni girl, who was forced into marriage, died during a painful childbirth that also killed her baby."[16]

It was a horrific story, but in the Islamic world, it was not an unusual one.

Another case in Yemen in 2008 had a happier outcome at first. An eight-year-old girl, Nojoud Mohammed, was granted a divorce from her thirty-year-old husband in a high-profile case. Gulf News reported at the time that Nojoud was joyful when she was granted her divorce:

"I am so happy to be free, and I will go back to school and will never think of getting married again," she said. "It is a good feeling to be rid of my husband and his bad treatment."[17]

The uniqueness of her case is that she was able to get a divorce at all, which is very rare in any of the Muslim countries.

In 2013, though, Nojoud said that her father withheld the money she should have been getting from the publishers of her story, has forced her out of the home, and has arranged for sister Haifa to marry a man twice her age. From the interview given by her to the *Guardian*, it seems that her ordeal is not yet over. Her concern is not only for herself, but for Haifa, who has now been married or sold at a very young age. It is very obvious that the father of these girls places no value on his daughters and is willing to marry them off for his own gain. When will the ordeal of these girls be over? When will anyone come to their aid?

In 2007, the International Centre for Research on Women reported that Yemen is one of twenty developing countries where child marriages are common. Nearly half of all Yemeni girls are married before the age of eighteen.

One Islamic country where child marriage is more common than any other place in the world is northern Nigeria, where Sharia law is enforced. The Nigerian government has tried to act against the practice, passing a law in 2003 entitled "The Child Rights Act" that set the minimum age for marriage at eighteen. Islamic clerics have been the fiercest opponents of the law.

Imam Sani, a Nigerian cleric, explained:

> "Child marriage in Islam is permissible; in the Quran, there is no specific age of marriage. Consequently, the Muslim clerics have a problem with the Child Rights Act and they decry it; they castigate it; they reject it; and they don't want it introduced in Nigeria. If the government imposes the law, there will be violent conflict from the Muslims, saying that no, we will not accept this; we'd rather die than accept something which is not a law from Allah."[18]

THE CATASTROPHE OF CHILD MARRIAGE

Throughout the world, there are many examples of desperate suffering and human tragedy as a result of child marriages.

A thirteen-year-old Yemeni child bride bled to death shortly after marriage; she was tied down and forced to have sex by her husband, according to the child's mother, police, and medical report. When discussing her child's injuries, the mother said her daughter looked as if she had been butchered.

In 2009, Elham Assi, thirteen, bled to death hours after she spoke to her mother and days after she was married to a twenty-three year-old man. She died in the deeply poor Yemeni village of Shueba, approximately two hundred kilometers northwest of the capital. Her husband, Abed al Hikmi, was placed in police custody. The practice of marrying young girls is widespread in Yemen, where a quarter of all females marry before the age of fifteen, according to a 2009 report by the country's Ministry of Social Affairs. Traditional families prefer young brides because they are seen as more obedient and are expected to have more children.[19]

And it is not over yet. In Iran, the legal age for marriage is nine for girls and fourteen for boys. The law has occasionally been exploited by pedophiles, who marry poor young girls from local provinces, abuse them, and then abandon them. In 2000, the Iranian parliament voted to raise the minimum age for girls to fourteen, but this past year, a legislative oversight body dominated by traditional clerics vetoed the edict. An attempt by conservatives to follow Yemen's lead to establish a legal minimum age of fifteen for girls failed, but local experts say it would rarely be enforced anyway.[20]

The Ayatollah Khomeini of Iran married a ten-year-old when he was twenty-eight . He called the marriage to a prepubescent girl "a divine blessing" and advised the faithful,

"Do your best to ensure that your daughters do not see their first blood in your house."[21]

An eight-year-old Saudi Arabian girl, who was married off by her father to a fifty-eight year old, was told that she cannot divorce her husband until she reaches puberty. Her lawyer, Abdu Jtili, said that the divorce petition was filed by the unnamed girl's divorced mother after the marriage contract was signed by her father and the groom. The judge dismissed the plea because the mother does not have the right to file, and ordered that the plea should be filed by the girl herself when she reaches puberty. The case was handled by a court in Qasim province, north of the Saudi capital Riyadh. The girl does not know she is married, said her lawyer, adding that he will appeal.[22]

In Nigeria, a federal court will hear a case over whether the West African nation's religious freedom and privacy laws allow a Muslim Senator to marry a thirteen-year-old girl, the latest rift in a country split between Christians and Muslims. The lawsuit filed by the Supreme Council for Sharia in Nigeria on behalf of Senator Ahman Sani Yerima challenges the country's child protection laws that ban women from marrying before the age of eighteen. The suit claims that Yerima's constitutional rights are being trampled over in the controversy surrounding his alleged marriage to a thirteen-year-old Egyptian girl. It is not the first time Yerima has apparently married a child. The Rights Commission alleged he married a fifteen-year-old girl only to divorce the young mother at seventeen. He told the BBC's Hausa Language Service that he considered "God's law and that of his Prophet above any other law...."[23]

The list of cases of child marriages could go on and on. These are innocent children who have no idea what will happen to them. They are often beaten and raped over and over again. Many suffer psychologically, physically, and emotionally. Many devout parents feel that they are acting according to Islamic law. Their thinking is that if Aisha could be happy in such a situation, their daughter should be also. The fault must lie with the child, not the abuser. This concept appears to be embraced by devout followers of Muhammad; it is simply Islamic culture, where bridal virginity is exploited by old men who lust at the sight of young, tender, untouched young girls.

Unfortunately, child brides younger than fifteen years old are five times more likely to die during childbirth or pregnancy than older women. Premature childbirth can lead to a variety of health problems, including fistula, a debilitating condition that causes chronic incontinence. Girls with this condition are often abandoned by their husbands and ostracized by society. Additionally, the young child brides suffer from domestic abuse and violence, causing post-traumatic stress and depression.[24]

A SUBTLE PRACTICE: FEMALE GENITAL MUTILATION

Forcing young girls into marriage to older men is not the only crimes that some Muslims commit. Many women are also victims of female circumcision. Islam leaves no option for these young women. They suffer physical trauma and emotional stress as a result of this inhumane procedure. There is much talk about this issue, which has opened up a Pandora's box for human rights organizations.

Female genital mutilation is the term used for the removal of all or a portion of the external female genitalia. There are three types of mutilation performed:

1. **Sunna or Traditional Circumcision**: Consists of the removal of the prepuce.

2. **Clitoridectomy**: Consists of removal of the entire clitoris.

3. **Infibulations**: Removal of all or part of the labia minora, the labia majora. This is then stitched up allowing a small hole to remain open to allow for urine and menstrual blood to flow through.[25]

There is no particular age set for this procedure. In general, female genital mutilation occurs between the ages of four and eight. Most of the time, this procedure is done without the assistance of medically-trained personnel (due to the lack of medical facilities in some of these countries). The use of anaesthesia is rare. The girls are held down by older women to prevent them from moving. Instruments used by the mid-wife will vary and could include any of the following: broken glass, a tin lid, razor blades, knives, scissors, or any other sharp object. Most of the time, there are no sterilization procedures. The result can be death, serious infections, abscesses, or hemorrhaging.[26]

The Qur'an is silent on this procedure, but we can find traces of female genital mutilation in the Hadiths. Muslim scholars who disapprove of this act claim that this practice is taken from a weak Hadith (one that does not necessarily rely on eyewitness accounts of historical events). On the other hand, some Muslim scholars agree to this practice and say that it has no side effects.

Farahat Sa'id Al Munju, Cleric of Al-Azhar (the top Islamic university), said on Al-Mihwar TV:

> "The Prophet said that circumcision is obligatory for men, and is NOBLE for women. This means that for the sake of her honor, a woman can be circumcised...."[27]

Muhammad's own words are recorded in Sunan Abu-Dawud:

> "When you circumcise, then do not cut severely, since that is better for her and more pleasing to the husband." Book 41, #5251, Hassan

Dr. Bilal Philips (Islam) said:

> "The practice in Sudan is mutilation while Islam is one hundred percent opposed to it! It is harmful to women, and many die in this process. Many have infections. Does Islam support or allow female circumcision? Yes! But on a very limited scale... very limited in practice...only the end of the clitoris...so it has no impact on feeling in the women. This is a basic practice that is permissible in Islam. The circumcision in Egypt, Sudan, and West African countries is an extreme view to ensure the virginity of the women involved...and it is from the pre-Islamic times. The harm that comes from all of this practice...Islam prohibits it."[28]

The World Health Organization (WHO) estimates that between 100 and 140 million women worldwide are currently circumcised, with about two million occurring each year. Most of these women live in twenty-eight African countries, as well as in Asia and the Middle East. The practice is internationally recognized as a violation of the human rights of girls and women.[29]

In Africa, female circumcisions occur from Senegal in West Africa to Ethiopia, on the east coast, as well as in Tanzania in the north and Sudan and Mali. The existence of this practice is also found in parts of Saudi Arabia, Jordan, Iraq, Egypt, Turkey, south Asia, and Iran. This issue has caused a great deal of debate among Islamic scholars. There are many who condemn it and believe that it is un-Islamic and brutal to women, yet at the same time, many others approve of it. It is also shocking to see that it is not only practiced in the aforementioned countries, but it is also becoming more common in European countries by Muslim immigrants. It is becoming more widely practised in Germany and the Netherlands, as well as Austria, where an estimated eight thousand immigrant girls are affected. In the U.K., it has been estimated that over twenty thousand girls under the age of fifteen are at risk of female genital mutilation in the U.K. each year and over sixty-six thousand women in the U.K. are living with the consequences of FMG.[30] Islamic religious leaders are encouraging Europe's Muslim Africans to follow Muhammad's recommendation of the ancient ritual involving the removal of the clitoris.

Understandably, many young girls find themselves filled with horror and hatred at the thought of genital mutilation. This brutal procedure is initiated by the parents themselves solely to reduce and control the sexual desire of the young daughter, thereby maintaining the honor, decency, and chastity of the child.

UP CLOSE AND PERSONAL

Last year, we took our daughter back to our country beause we truly wanted her to experience living in an Islamic country. She came to the U.S.A. when she was five and had no recollection of her life there. This is her own account of her experiences and her feelings about her trip:

"I am privileged to share my experience living in a Muslim country with you all. My visit has being an interesting and very intensive one. I learned how different this world is, how scary and how strange it can seem. Though I was briefed about the culture that is surrounded by the Islamic religion of this land, I now am living it—especially how to dress, how to behave, and how to act in public as a girl. When I first got here, I didn't like it at all because I had no freedom. I was trapped in the four boundaries of my grandma's house and only allowed to leave when I was chaperoned by my uncle, aunts, or mom. I had to cover my head and my chest with a long veil (looks like a long scarf). I wore a long shirt and something that looked like loose pants before I could go out.

"There were times when I got so depressed that things didn't go the way I wanted to. It was then I was comforted by my mother's warm and loving hugs. Crying in secrecy was my only outlet. My heart goes out to those children, especially girls, who have no hope of any freedom. In all honesty, they are flightless birds that are caged. If you were to see it with your own eyes, you would know what I am talking about. I wish you could also see, touch, and feel the oppression that I have seen in their eyes. As an American, we cannot comprehend it because we see so much freedom, but we will realize it when we live it."

After returning back to the U.S., our daughter appreciates the freedom she has here more than before. Although she has apprehensions about returning back to her birth country because of the oppression felt in the air, she feels strongly that if it will be the Lord's will for her to return, then His will must be done in her life.

End Notes

1) Princess by Jean Sasson Pg 59.

2) www.wikipedia encyclopedia.com.

3) Quran 2:24.

4) www.Islamwomen.com/marriage/intro_to_marraige.php.

5) Hadiths: Sahih Bukhari 9-86:100; Sahih Bukhari 9-86:101

6) Sahih Bukhari 9-85:79. www.wikiislam.com/wiki/Quran, Hadiths and scholars: women.

7) www.islamreview.blogspot.Aisha-Ayesha. The child bride of Muhammad.

8) www.answering-islam.org/silas/childbride.htm. Muhammad, Aisha, Islam and child Bride.

9) Courtesy of Memri TV, Sat, March 29, 2008, Television clip of Sharia Expert.

10) www.wikiislam.net/wikicontemporary-pedophilic-Islamic-marriage: by Jenny Cuff: child marriage and divorce in Yemen BBC, Nov 6, 2008.

11) Top Saudi Cleric: OK for a young girl to wed: CNN, Jan 17, 2009.

12) Ayatollah Khomeini's Religious Teachings on Marriage, Divorce and Relationships by Parvin Darabi. Dr Homa Daraboo foundation.

13) Saudi Marriage official says one-year-old bride OK: Fox News, June 2, 2008 interview on LBC-TV.

14) Child Bride in the Islamic World, Robert Spencer, Front Page Magazine: Sep 18,2009.

15) Islamists Fight Yemen Law Banning Child Marriage: foxnews, April 2009.

16) FreeThoughtNation.com/...Islam-disturbing-legacy-of–slavery.

17) Article. CNN.com/.../Yemen, childbirth, death. Sep. 14, 2009 by Muhammad Jamjoon.

18) Front Page Magazine: Child Marriage in the Islamic world: Sep. 18, 2009 by Robert Spencer.

19) Ibid. Pg 35.

20) The women of Islam, Time Magazine: Nov. 25, 2001 by Lisa Beyer.

21) The Spirit Of Allah: Khomeini and Islamic Revolution, Adler and Adler, 1986, Pg 90-91.

22) www.guardian.co.uk/world/2008/...Saudi-Arabia-human-rights.

23) www.jihadwatch.org/.../Nigeria-marriage of Muslim-Senator-to-13-ys-old-girl.

24) www.pbs.org/now/show/341/fact/html-Child Bride-Child Marriages, What we now know, PBS.

25) www.members.tripod.com/wolves/dreams/FGM.html. Female Genital Mutilation.

26) Ibid.

27) www.jihadwatch.org/.../female-genital-mutilation-is-part-of-the sunna-of-the-prophet.

28) www.schnellmann.org/female-circumsion.

29) www.who.net.int/mediacentre/factsheet/fs2.

30) www.nhs.UK/conditions/female-genital-mutilation/Pg/introduction.aspx.

Chapter 4
The Obedient Muslim Wife

The systematic abuse of women in Muslim countries around the world has prompted concern by many human rights activists. Much is being done to find justice for those who are victims of domestic violence. However, in spite of the many efforts to quell this abuse, brutality still continues. The problem seems to stem from an ideology that is more potent than we could ever imagine and is based on what Muslims believe are the eternal and unchangeable words of the Qur'an and the Hadiths.

Women living under the laws of Sharia are unable to free themselves from this written bondage. They do not know, nor have they experienced, what it means to be living in a free country. From time to time, several women may have raised their voices in protest against the brutality, and to some extent, they have been successful. However, these short-lived protests have not lasted. They were silenced by the sword of Islam: fear. Standing against Islamic law, Sharia, can lead to their grave. If they are not tracked down by their own family members, they will no doubt be hunted down by members of the Umma (the Muslim community).

Many Muslims living in the West claim that Islam respects and provides equal rights to women; they simply do not know or understand the Qur'an very well. There are moderate Muslims who really do support equal rights for women, but on the whole, many Muslims are silent. Some may say they support equal rights simply in order to show Islam in a good light to western people, while denying those rights to a Muslim audience. Such deception is called Al-Taqquiya, and is considered justifiable in the struggle to spread Islam. Why are women in Muslim countries subjected to so much abuse? Why are the men in their lives so abusive? Is the protection a woman receives in Islam as claimed by these men true or fabricated? The Qur'an teaches that men may chastise their wives physically. This is hardly ever mentioned in the West whereas many articles are written claiming that Islam has raised the status of women and protects and honors them. The real situation reveals a different picture.

The Qur'an clearly states:

> "Men are in charge of women, because Allah hath made the one of them to excel the other, and because they spend [sic] their property (for the support of women). So good women are obedient, guarding in secret that which Allah hath guarded. As for those from whom ye fear rebellion, admonish them and banish them to beds apart; and scourge (beat) them. Then if they obey you, seek not a way against them. Lo! Allah is ever High Exalted, Great."[1]

Countless numbers of cases of women being beaten by their husbands are reported each year. These women will carry physical and emotional scars for the rest of their lives.

In 2000, I went to visit my mother for Christmas. During my visit, I found out that my husband and I were expecting our first child. My mom took me to the gynaecologist for a routine check-up. While waiting for my turn, a young woman was rushed in on a gurney screaming in pain and bleeding heavily. The quiet waiting area became a place of chaos, as all the medical personnel rushed into the emergency room. Her relatives, restrained from following her, were left sobbing in the waiting room. My mother rushed into the emergency room to offer assistance and quickly returned to question the young girl's family. As she listened, her expression gradually changed from concern to disbelief and dismay.

When she returned to my side, Mom explained that the family had told her the seventeen-year-old had been married the previous night; her husband was a stranger picked out by the family. At her new husband's advances, the young bride became fearful and resisted his touch. This enraged him, and he forced himself on her, cruelly raping her. Observing her refusal of his advances, he kicked her several times in the lower abdomen, the blows so violent that her uterus was ruptured. When she started bleeding profusely he called his family to take her to the hospital, telling them that he had taught her a lesson and that she would not repeat her mistake in the future.

Hearing this story caused my own stomach to cramp severely; we left the hospital without my having a check-up. We do not know what happened to the young bride; however, my mother did tell me that the doctors were still trying to stabilize her as she fought for her life.

Was the husband wrong in what he did to his bride of one day? Not according to Muslims, since the law favors the husband. It was the woman's fault; she should have been submissive to his demands. If a husband calls his wife to bed, can she say no? Does not the Qur'an teach; "that a husband has the right to have sex with his wife by force; you can enjoy a wife by force..."?

Sahih Al-Bukhari and Sahih Muslim both say:

> "When a man calls his wife for sexual intimacy and she refuses him, thus he spends the night in anger, and then the angels curse her until morning."[2]

The following sayings demonstrate that a wife must always be sexually compliant with her husband's demands:

> "A wife should not refuse her husband if he wants to enjoy her body. If the wife of a man dies while he is pleased with her, she will enter Paradise. If a man wants sex, his wife must comply with him even if she is on the back of a camel. A woman cannot keep optional fast without her husband's permission. If she does God will not accept her fast." Ghazali volume 2, p.43

> "Allah gets displeased with the woman who does not immediately respond when her husband demands sex from her."[3]

Women know that they need to live according to Islamic law. A woman knows that she must fulfill her husband's sexual desires even when she is not in the mood or may not be feeling well. She will probably have a sleepless night if she fears she will be cursed by an angel, as the Muslim scriptures tells her:

"The angels curse a woman for refusing to have sex with her husband...." Sahih Bukhari 4.54.460

Muslim nations are considered patriarchies; that is to say, men are in the dominant position of power, forcing the women into a submissive, weak, and often exploited role. In the name of Islam, the Muslim male thinks nothing of oppressing and abusing the Muslim woman; it is a way of life practiced by most husbands. Basically, the men do not believe they are doing anything wrong, since they are following the teachings of their faith. The Qur'an and the Hadiths make this abundantly clear, as can be seen from the following teachings:

> "Men are protectors and maintainers of women; women must be devoutly obedient, if not, beat them." Qur'an 4:34

> "A man will not be asked as to why he beats his wife. A woman who complains about the beating she receives from her husband is not the best woman." Sunaan Abu Dawud 11.2142

This verse means, in essence, that a woman has no right to share her feelings with her husband or object in any way about her treatment at his hand.

The next verse also endorses her punishment.

> "...As to those women on whose part ye fear disloyalty and ill conduct, admonish them, refuse to share their beds, and beat them." Sura an Nisa 4:34

Iyas-B-Abdullah reported that the Messenger of Allah said, "Don't beat the maids of Allah." Then Omar came to Muhammad and said, "Women have become daring against their husbands."

So Muhammad allowed them to beat them. The Hadith then states:

> "that women began to lay siege on Muhammad to mediate their beatings."

The correctness of beating wives is approved by Muhammad, who also seems to imply that the husband gets pleasure from such beatings. Omar reported from the holy prophet who said, "No man shall be questioned for beating his wife." In the very next Hadith, a woman complained to Muhammad that her husband beat her while she prayed. Muhammad told her to change her time of prayer or pray shorter prayers so that her husband could get on with the joy of beating her.[4]

DISCIPLINARY MEASURES

Corporal punishment has become an abusive and often common way of life for Muslim men as a punishment for taming their wives, and Muslim women continue to be physically abused, oppressed, and victimized in the twenty-first century. This situation exists not only in Muslim nations, but sometimes also in the West.

In Pakistan, women face discrimination on a daily basis. Various forms of domestic violence in the country include beating, honor killings, spousal abuse including marital rape, acid attacks, and being set afire by family members. These crimes are often ignored by society and by law enforcers.

The Pakistan Institute of Medical Sciences has determined that over ninety percent of Pakistani wives have been beaten and abused sexually, even for such minor offences as cooking unsavory meals. Many are punished for failing to give birth to a male child.[5]

This book will not have enough room to record the many documented cases of abuse. However, some of the more violent incidents of domestic abuse have taken place most particularly in the following regions discussed below.

First we will see what is happening in the fortress of Islam...

Islamabad, Pakistan

Nicholas Kristof wrote an article in *The New York Times* about a woman in Pakistan who was disfigured after acid was thrown on her by her husband who was angered because of her decision to file for a divorce.

Naeema Azar, an attractive and self-confident real estate agent, had decided to divorce her husband, Azar Jamsheed, a fruit seller who rarely brought home any money. Azar agreed to end his marriage because he had his eye on another woman. After the divorce was finalized, he stopped by the house one day to say goodbye to his children. Pulling out a bottle of acid, he threw it in his wife's face.

Ms. Azar recalled, "I screamed. The flesh on my cheeks was falling off. The bones on my face were showing, and all of my skin was falling off!"

Kristof added, "The most haunting part of the story was an encounter by her twelve-year-old son, Ahsan Shah, who lovingly leads her around everywhere. He noted that in one house where they stayed for a time after the attack, a man accustomed to beating his wife regularly taunted her with, 'You see the woman downstairs who was burned by her husband? I will burn you the same way!'"[6]

The *Times* reporter noted that Mr. Jamsheed was never arrested and has since disappeared. Ms. Azar is being supported by the Ms. Bukhara Group, a Progressive Women's Association, which is paying for eye surgery to restore sight to one eye. The Bukhari Group has documented 7,800 cases of women in Islamabad alone who were deliberately subjected to acid attacks, burned, or scalded. Only two percent of the assailants in these cases were convicted of their crimes.

What does the 'caring' Taliban (whose name means "seekers of truth") have to say?

Kabul, Afghanistan

Shameen remains traumatized as she recounts the event that led her to her present life in a safe-house in Kabul. She had suffered daily beatings after marrying as a teenager. She had been tortured and abused, often with electrical wiring or a hammer.

Shameen and her husband could not conceive a child. In Afghan society, the blame generally falls on the woman if the married couple is unable to have a child. After one severe beating, Shameen ran away from home to the police. When her husband came for her, he promised he would not attack her again, so she gave in and went home with him.

Days later, Shameen's husband took her on a trip to visit her sister's grave, a fifteen-year-old girl who was burned to death for displeasing her husband. Her younger sister was only eleven years old when she was forced to marry an older man. He beat and abused her until the day he eventually killed her.

Shameen's husband took her to her sister's shrine where he forced her to the ground, lifted her burqa (veil), and raped her. Then he threatened her with a knife and began slashing her throat and body. A passerby saved her, but she had no one to turn to—not even her parents. In their eyes, Shameen had brought them shame, an offense punishable by death. The honor of the family is of over-riding importance in this Muslim nation.

Shameen now lives in the shelter run by Women for Afghan Women (WAW). This shelter houses fifty-four women and children.

According to the United Nations Development Office, nearly ninety percent of all Afghan women suffer at the hands of the men in their lives.[7]

Surely Al-Qaeda views a woman differently in...

Baghdad, Iraq

Mays Adnan feels she is lucky to have survived years of beatings, harassment, and humiliation at the hands of her husband.

"I spent ten years being beaten by my husband and had two abortions due to the violence," the thirty-six-year-old primary school teacher admitted in a recent interview. "I was threatened by my father that if I divorced my husband I would be killed." She finally had to resort to seeking support from a women's advocacy group to help her.

According to activists and international reports, many Iraqi women suffer violence at the hands of their husbands, parents, or other relatives.

"In northern and southern Iraq, women are victims of daily violence," states Hadeel Athab, a women's activist and aid worker/volunteer at a local NGO. "There was an official number of questionable suicide cases numbering around 120 in the second half of last year; but our research has shown that that number might be as many as 240 cases of suicide in Iraq," says Athab.[8]

A recent report by the United Nations Assistance Mission of Iraq (UNAMI) registered 139 cases of violence against women in the northern region of Kurdistan in the second half of 2008. The report also stated that 163 women were killed as a result of domestic violence in Kurdistan in 2009. Law experts agree that neither the authorities nor the laws offer any protection to women against domestic violence within Muslim nations.[9]

Who stands for women in Palestine?

Abuse in Palestine

A Palestinian woman named Sanaa Umar was married at fifteen and divorced at the age of sixteen. "My husband started beating me without any reason the second week of the marriage," says Sanaa, who is now seventeen.

"He beat me with a stick all over my body. It was like he was controlled by a genie. Even his own mother tried to stop him, but she couldn't."

Her father had arranged the marriage with her twenty-two-year-old husband. Even after the marriage, Sanaa's husband continued a relationship with another fifteen-year-old whose father had forbidden the marriage. At one point, Sanaa was beaten so badly that she was unable to get out of bed for a week. Eventually, her husband dumped her at her father's house, where she now lives while attending school to become a hairdresser.

This situation is all too common in Gaza, where more than one in five women say they suffer from domestic violence, yet there is not a single women's shelter where these women can seek refuge. Could this be a matter of security? The Human Rights Watch (HRW) condemns the Palestinian police and justice system for the near-total failure to protect women in both Gaza and the West Bank from abuses, including rape, incest, beatings, and "honor killings." In most cases of abuse, the justice system rules in favor of the man. Only one percent of polled Palestinian women said that they had lodged complaints against the offenders, and of the eighty-five reported cases of rape in 2003, only one case resulted in a conviction! There have been ninety-eight officially reported cases of honor killing and/or domestic cases of murder of Gaza women in the West Bank since 2000.[10]

What does moderate Islam say about abuse against women?

Abuse in Turkey

For the past forty years, Turkey has been attempting to join the European Union. As the country has worked to become a member, it has still failed to show its citizens the path to civilization. Violence and abuse toward women are now at record high numbers. According to the tally taken by Bianet, which reviewed newspaper articles, Internet sites, and news agencies during the entire 2010 year, Turkish men had murdered 217 women and three children; injured 164 women and four children; harassed 381 women and children; and raped 207 women and children.[11]

The majority of harassment and rape victims were children. Twenty-three women died of alleged suicide (or under suspicious circumstances). At least 646 men and boys were taken into custody for alleged murder, injury, harassment, and rape.

Fifty percent of the women murdered in 2010 were killed by their husbands, while thirteen percent were murdered by boyfriends, eleven percent by fathers, eight percent by divorced husbands, and four percent by siblings (brothers) and/or other relatives.[12]

Where are the feminist advocates?

Abuse of Muslim Women in the West

Perhaps you are wondering if these tragic incidences take place only in the Muslim world. We need to understand how difficult it is for a Muslim to separate from his faith and cultural upbringing. We also need to understand that those who commit such crimes feel that they are simply following Allah's commandments. Such practices do not weigh heavily on the individual, but rather on the shoulders of the family and the community. The ideology of Islam, no matter where it is found in the world, has a dedicated following. Therefore, it should come as no surprise that the practices of Islam reach into our own backyard in the United States and other Western nations.

In the process of writing this book, I read many blogs written by Muslims from Syria, Egypt, Turkey, and other countries. The one recurring sentiment in these blogs was explicit bitterness against the West, attacking western nations in regard to the abuse of their women. Such a reaction is quite natural when a group's ideology is brought into question; it is natural to feel intimidated and lash out with facts to convince others that abuse by Christian men also exists in the West. The question is how many preachers are encouraging their congregations to beat their wives. The Bible gives us a description of marriage in Hebrews 13:4:

> "Marriage is honourable in all, and the bed undefiled…"

The Bible never states that it is permissible to abuse a woman or a wife. On the contrary, it is recorded in the Qur'an, as well as in the Hadiths, that husbands have the right to batter their wives.

Sahih Bukhari states:

> "A woman came to Muhammad and begged him to stop her husband from beating her. Her skin was bruised so badly that it is described as being greener than the green veil she was wearing.

Muhammad did not admonish her husband, but instead ordered her to return to him and submit to his sexual desires."[13]

While recently visiting a church in North Carolina, I had the opportunity to share my insights on the life of a woman living in a Muslim country. After the class, a woman walked up to me and wanted to share her story. She wept as she told me that she had been married to a Muslim man in the U.S. and now, after fifteen years, had filed for divorce, as well as for custody of the children. She explained how she was beaten and abused and yet, out of love, had suffered at his hands, always hoping that one day he might change. Her love for him and her silence were all in vain, and when the situation finally became impossible to bear, she gave up. Her heart had become so bitter towards any Middle Eastern man who looked at her that she refused even to talk to my husband.

My point in sharing this episode is to again show that it is not where the Muslim man is living that affects his behavior toward his wife, but rather it is the irrational teachings of the Qur'an that encourage him to abuse a woman. This can be seen from the remarks of some prominent Muslims in Europe and the USA.

In 2004, an Imam from Spain named Mohammed Kamal Mustafa was found guilty of "inciting violence on the basis of gender" for his book, *Women in Islam*, which discussed the methods and limits of administering physical punishment on a woman. Additionally, a prominent American Muslim leader, Dr. Muzammil H. Siddiqi, the former president of the Islamic Society of North America (ISNA), has said that:

"in some cases a husband may use some light disciplinary action in order to correct the moral infraction of his wife.....the Koran is very clear on this issue."[14]

Sheikh Yousef Qaradhawi, one of the most respected and influential Islamic clerics in the world, wrote:

"If the husband senses that feelings of disobedience and rebelliousness are rising against him in his wife, he should try his best to rectify her attitude by kind words, gentle persuasion, and reasoning with her. If this is not helpful, he should sleep apart from her, trying to awaken her agreeable feminine nature so that serenity may be restored, and she may respond to him in a harmonious fashion. If this approach fails, it is permissible for him to beat her lightly with his hand, avoiding her face and other sensitive part."[15]

The question here is, does Islam contribute toward the restoration of women's dignity and rights? Does a woman have to live continually under the fear of Allah who commands his followers to be ready to beat her at any moment for minor disobedience? How can Muslims say that they are the protectors of their women when evidence shows clearly that she is viewed as being of less value than any man?

At this point, I would like to confess that I am so grateful to the Lord Jesus Christ who promised me never to forsake me in my weaknesses. Thus, His Holy Spirit and grace constantly remind me who I am in Him and that His mercies are new every day. I do not have to live in fear of any potent ideology to suffer abuse or feel that I am worthless in His sight.

End Notes

1) Quran 4:34.

2) See: Riyad Al-Salihin, #281.

3) Sahih-Al-Bukhari 4-54:460/7- 62:81/8-3367:3368.

4) Al-Hadis,Vol 1,Pg 212 (65).

5) Briefing: Violence against women in Pakistan, April 17, 2002: www.web. amnesty.org/ai.nsf/index/ASA 330203003.

6) Op-Ed Columist, Terrorism That's Personal. www.NYTimes.com/2008/ 11/30/opinion.

7) Atia Abawi, "Afghan Women Hiding For Their Lives," CNN, Sep. 24, 2009.

8) 208.43.71.196-static.reverse.softlayer.com/English /News/.../425622.

9) Afif Sarhan, Iraq's Domestic Violence Plight, Islam Online, May 31, 2009.

10) www.independent.co.uk/news/World/Middle East/ abuse of women still rife in Palestinian life, D Macintyre, Nov 06.

11) Rojwomen.com/2011/...217-women-killed-by-men-in Turkey-in 2010.

12) Ibid.

13) Sahih Bukhari 72:715

14) www.thewomenofislam.blogspot.com/2011/02/Feb 13, 2011.

15) Memri.org/March25,2004: www.ummah.com/forum/showthreat. php33857-Islam-s

Chapter 5
In the Name of Honor

The tragedy of women living under the umbrella of Islam goes on and on. Hundreds of women are being slaughtered by their own family members. These hideous crimes are often committed by fathers, brothers, uncles, and even, on several occasions, by mothers themselves.

What would you do if you discovered that your wife, daughter, or niece was engaged in a pre-marital or extra-marital relationship? As a father, mother, uncle, aunt, or grandparent, would you condemn them and pick up the first stone, or would you ask God's wisdom and guidance in helping you deal with the situation, offering Scriptural truth and explaining the teaching of the Bible?

Most of us have heard the term "honor killings." Honor killings not only occur regularly in the Middle East and South Asia, but also now in Europe and North America. These crimes are happening either because the woman is suspected of, or has actually committed, a sin, violating the family honor. The Muslim family depends on the sexual purity of its female members. A violation can occur if the woman speaks to an unrelated man, if there is rumor of pre-marital loss of virginity or an extra-marital affair, if a woman refuses a forced marriage, if a woman marries someone not acceptable to the family, or if a woman has been raped. Once honor is lost or polluted, it becomes mandatory for the family to "cleanse or purify" themselves by spilling the blood of the woman who has brought dishonor to the family. Those who carry out the honor killings in Muslim countries are usually given a light sentence when brought before the courts and, in most cases, are not even judged. The offenders are considered not guilty because the killing was carried out in accordance with their Islamic beliefs.

Family honor is a core value in a Muslim household today. Its roots can be traced back to pre-Islamic Arab societies. Pre-Islamic tribes committed many hideous crimes in the name of honor, including the uncivilized practices of stoning, flogging, beheading, torture, and slavery. Today's Muslims have incorporated most of these inhumane pagan practices into their lives, which they now refer to as Allah's law.[1]

Whenever a Muslim is questioned in the West about any of these practices, he will defend himself by lying, saying that this is not Islam. Muslims portray Islam as peaceful and respectful of their women. We Westerners tend to believe what they want us to believe. However, the Qur'an and Hadiths tell us what the unchangeable words of Allah and Muhammad have said. The following verses show that imprisonment and death are the penalties for any sexual misbehavior on a woman's part:

> "If any of your women are guilty of lewdness, take the evidence of four (reliable) witnesses from amongst you against them; then confine them to houses until death do claim them. Or God ordain for them some (other) way." Qur'an 4:15

It is interesting that although the horrific killing by stoning is a very common practice in the Muslim world, there is no verse in the Qur'an that sanctions the punishment. However the evidence is present in the Hadiths, considered by Muslim scholars to be the undisputed compilation of their prophet's traditions.

This Hadith tells the story of a woman seeking forgiveness for adultery:

> "...A woman came to the Prophet and asked for purification by seeking punishment. He told her to go away and seek God's forgiveness. She persisted four times and admitted she was pregnant. He told her to wait until she had given birth. Then he said that the Muslim community should wait until she weaned her child. When the day arrived for the child to take solid food, Muhammad handed the child over to the community. And when he had given command over her and she was put in a hole up to her breast, he ordered the people to stone her. Khalid bal Walid came forward with a stone, which he threw at her head, and when the blood spurted on her face, he cursed her." Sahih Muslim Book 017, # 4206

The Saudi Ambassador to London, Ghazi al-Qusaibi, remarks that stoning may seem irrational to the Western mind, but it is "at the core of the Islamic faith." An intellectual, the Saudi ambassador asserted that stoning adulterers to death is a legitimate punishment for society. He also stated that Westerners should respect Muslim culture on this matter.[2]

Sheikh Ahmad Kutty, a senior lecturer and Islamic scholar at the Islamic Institute of Toronto, Canada, states:

"Adultery in Islam is one of the most heinous and deadliest of sins. Its enormity can be gauged from the fact that it has often been conjoined in the Qur'an with gravest of all sins; shirk or associating partners with Allah."[3]

Al Skudsi bin Hookah, roving reporter and foreign correspondent for the *Gaza Gajee*, expresses his support for honor killing:

"I am very unhappy. Our way of life is under attack. And we are not fighting back. Deep down, we know that when a woman has disgraced her family, nothing will restore honor except by killing her. This is understood in Jordan, Syria, Yemen, Lebanon, Egypt, the Gaza strip, and the West Bank. So why are we Arabs telling the Western press that honor killing is cultural, that it is not really part of Islam? Our way of life is based on maintaining our honor. And make no mistake about it: a woman does tarnish her family's honor by engaging in pre-marital sex, by getting herself raped, when she seeks divorce, and when she marries against her family's wishes. And keeping our women pure is a big part of our honor. So there's no point in saying honor killing isn't really part of our religion. Honor and Islam are inextricably bound; they are what give our life meaning. A strong religion demands we choose to maintain our honor."[4]

Bassam al Hadid, a Jordanian with an American doctorate who spent twelve years as a hospital administrator in the United States, said:

> "I would do what I have to do," when asked whether he would kill a daughter who had sex outside a marriage.[5]

The United Nations estimates that there are over 5,000 honor killings annually. They take place in Bangladesh, Brazil, Ecuador, Egypt, India, Israel, Italy, Jordan, Pakistan, Morocco, Sweden, Turkey, United Kingdom, and Uganda. Countries not reporting honor killings, but who are perhaps the largest violators of women's rights, include Afghanistan, Iraq, Iran, and the territories of Palestine.[6]

Muslim women believe that submitting to the will of Allah will save them and hopefully afford them a slim chance of entering Paradise. There is a verse that speaks of obedience to a husband as being the essential criterion for a woman to enter Paradise. Therefore, they submit to Allah's will, to their husbands, and to the abuse they receive. This is categorized as "obedience." They have nothing left but to turn to their so-called heavenly and earthly "protectors." Although full of doubt, they silently and secretly pray and hope for salvation. Their men, pretending to be faithful Muslims, have no remorse or fear of punishment; they feel compelled to kill an erring woman in accordance with the commands of Allah.

Muslim women have grown accustomed to living with fear, spending their lives imprisoned in their own homes. Fears mount as one wrong move could possibly be their last one. They have desires and dreams like all women, but they are unable to even daydream about them. The women fear beautifying themselves with makeup or perfume because it is written in the Hadith:

> "Allah's messenger (may peace be upon him) as saying: Every eye is lustful, and when a woman applies perfume and then goes about in an assembly, she is like such and such, i.e., adulteress." Al-Tirmidhi, Hadiths 1065 Narrated by Abu Musa.

She lives with the fear that if she is raped, she will not be able to produce four witnesses to prove her plight.

Islam not only has a biased opinion, but it also lacks common sense. Logic says, Why would anyone rape a woman in front of other people? The worse scenario is that if she complains or presses charges against the rapist, she in turn will be charged with making a false accusation. Whether she likes it or not, she has nowhere to escape but to face the ultimate sentence: her death. It is rare to find any rape case in which a sentence is handed down in favor of the woman. Most of the time, even after being brutally raped, a woman may also be falsely charged under Islamic law for allowing the rape to occur, which most likely will result in a sentence of death by execution.

One such bizarre case involved a seven-year-old girl in Tehran, Iran, whose father, Khazir, beheaded her because he suspected that she had been raped by her uncle. He said that he acted "to defend my honor, fame, and dignity."[7]

Again, common sense tells us that any seven year old would not be an adulterous woman. Who can change the historic words from beloved Muhammad's mouth and of the unaltered directions from Allah? Allah's decree for fornicators clearly dictates dreadful punishment for illicit sexual intercourse, as can be seen in the Qur'an 24:2:

> "The [unmarried] woman or [unmarried] man found guilty of sexual intercourse—lash each one of them with a hundred lashes, and do not be taken by pity for them in the religion of Allah, if you should believe in Allah and the Last Day. And let a group of the believers witness their punishment."

Due to the strictness of the Islamic law, there are currently no Islamic governments who dare to ban the practices of the beating and slaughtering of innocent young girls and women. This butchering, stoning, flogging, beheading, or hanging is usually not carried out privately, but often becomes public entertainment. The whole community enjoys watching and sometimes even takes part in the execution. Public punishment proves that the shame has been cleansed from the family and is a strong warning to the spectators, especially the women and children, that they dare not take that dreadful step themselves. Shockingly, during these executions, parents often join in killing their own flesh and blood. Unfortunately, millions of people are silent the world over, pretending not to know what is happening in the Muslim world. No one dares to object to these practices.

For a Muslim woman, her faith is the invisible threat that leads her to her destiny. Islam has no room for compassion or the value of human life. The rules of this "peaceful" religion are based on cruelty, manipulation, and fear—fear of Allah, who takes pleasure in slaughtering innocent lives, using men as pawns. Everyone, especially women, live in constant fear of the anger of the "merciful" Allah.

All over the Muslim world, there are heart-rending stories of the suffering of defenseless Muslim women. Sometimes women themselves take part in killing their daughters, claiming that family honor is at stake.

In Pakistan, for example, Samia Sarward, was shot dead in her lawyer's office where she had gone to meet her mother. Her mother had enabled the killer to gain access to the meeting by insisting that she had trouble walking and needed Samia's husband to assist her. The murder was planned by the mother, a medical doctor; her father, a well-known businessman and head of the Chamber of Commerce; and her aunt. Samia was married to her cousin, and after suffering abuse from her husband, she had decided to get a divorce.

In the meantime, she had fallen in love with an Army Captain and requested her family's permission to marry him, even though her divorce from her cousin had not become final. When her family denied her request to remarry, she eloped with her Captain, escaping to Lahore, a province of Punjab. When she ran out of money, she tried to contact her relatives, who, in turn, informed her parents as to her whereabouts. Samia was living in a woman's shelter in Lahore waiting for her divorce to become finalized. Her mother then tricked her into thinking her family had accepted her relationship with her new love. Once the mother met Samia in the attorney's office, the murderer pulled out a gun and killed Samia.[8]

In Palestine, Amira Abu Hanhan Qaoud murdered her daughter, Rofayda Qaoud, who had been raped by her brother and had become pregnant. Armed with a plastic bag, a razor, and a wood stick, Amira entered her sleeping daughter's room, saying, "Tonight you die, Rofayda," before wrapping the bag tightly around Rofayda's head. Amira slit her daughter's wrists, ignoring the muffled pleas of "No, mother, no!" After her daughter went limp, Amira, the forty-three-year-old mother of nine, struck the daughter with the stick saying, "I had to protect my other children. This is the only way I could protect my family's honor."[9]

Other family members, too, such as brothers, cousins, fathers, or uncles, take on the role of protecting the family by punishing any who step out of line. In Jordan, a brother drowned his twenty-two-year-old sister, who was having an extramarital affair. The charge was that the unidentified woman's brother beat her with the help of his family and then took her to the Dead Sea where he drowned her. Her parents and another brother were charged with assisting in her murder.[10]

Simply talking with a man on Facebook resulted in a young woman being brutally murdered. A Saudi woman was murdered by her father due to a Muslim Cleric's criticism of Facebook, the Internet social networking site. This case, as reported by Saudi Arabian News, was cited as an example of the trouble that Facebook has caused in Saudi Arabia. The site had become controversial after the Cleric had labeled it a destructive force against Islam.

"Facebook is a door to lust, and young women and men are spending more on their phones and the Internet than they are spending on food," the Cleric said. Jihad Watch reported that the Riyadh woman was beaten and shot by her father after he discovered she engaged in an online conversation with a man on the website.[11]

In Iraq, the violent killing of a young girl by her father went unpunished. After all, she had stepped outside the boundaries of Islamic laws, and her honour killing was considered justifiable. The seventeen-year-old girl was murdered by her father in an honour killing after falling in love with a British soldier, whom she had met while working for an aid program in Basra. Rand Abdel-Qader was stomped upon, suffocated, and stabbed by her father. She was then given an unceremonious burial to emphasize her disgrace. Her father was released after he was arrested.

Sergeant Ali Jabbar of the Basra Police said, "Not much can be done when we have an honor killing case. You are in a Muslim society, and women should live under religious laws. The father has very good contacts inside the Basra government, and it wasn't hard for him to be released and for what he did to be forgotten."

Ms. Qader, a student of English at Basra University, had struck up a friendship with the twenty-two-year-old British infantryman when he was delivering relief packages to displaced families. The young Muslim woman was a volunteer worker for the program.[12]

For some young women, the cause of their murder is not love but leaving the Muslim faith and converting to Christianity. In Somalia, Nurta Mohammad Farah, age seventeen, was shot in the chest and head by a family member for converting to Christianity. When her parents found out about her new faith, they offered her forgiveness if she would renounce her faith. Nurta was kept in shackles and locked in a dark room while being treated for mental illness. She was able to flee, but was then discovered. When family members found out that she would not denounce Christ, they killed her.[13]

However, not all of these honor killings take place in Middle Eastern settings. Some have taken place much closer to home, and the incidents are on the rise. In Europe, the USA, and Canada, there is an increasing awareness of such crimes.

An appalling case in Buffalo, New York, drew a great deal of media attention. Muzzammil Hassan, who was forty-four years old, allegedly and cold-bloodedly beheaded his wife, Aasiya, who was thirty-seven, at Bridges TV, the Muslim-based cable network's office. Ironically, the cable network was founded by Hassan in 2004 to combat the negative perceptions of Muslims claimed to be dominant in mainstream media coverage. Hassan apparently committed the crime the week after Aasiya started divorce proceedings.

Hassan founded Bridges TV upon the inspiration of his wife saying, "Some derogatory comments were being made about Muslims that offended her. She was seven months pregnant, and she thought she didn't want her kids growing up in this environment." Bridges TV originally declared that its intentions were to "infuse American culture with the values of Islam in a healthy, family-oriented way."

A local professor named Faizan Haq, who helped Hassan launch Bridges TV, declared, "I think Aasiya is a martyr. She has given her life to protect the image of American Muslims, and as an American Muslim community, we owe it to her not to let this happen again."[14]

Aasiya's crime was that she was filing for a divorce from her abusive husband in order to live out the rest of her life in peace. Oddly, Hassan calls himself a moderate Muslim. So, if he is moderate, how could he commit such a hideous crime? This type of behaviour is what you would expect from an extremist. Sadly, Muslims living in the United States did not openly discuss this issue, nor did any condemn it.

The need to exercise complete control over female members of the family can bring tensions with young daughters who see Western ways and begin to resent the restrictions placed upon them. In Ontario, Canada, the male members of one family, whose sixteen-year-old daughter was rebelling, objected to her behaviour, which resulted in her murder. She was killed by her father, who later called the police and confessed. The young girl was strangled for refusing to wear the traditional head covering, the hijab. During the father's murder trial, the Superior Court Justice acknowledged that the slaying was an Islamic honor killing stating, "I find it profoundly disturbing that a sixteen year old could be murdered by a father and brother for the purpose of saving family pride and for saving them from what they perceived as a family embarrassment."[15]

A similar case in Dallas, Texas, involved an Egyptian-born taxi driver, Yaser Abdel Said, who cold-bloodedly killed his two daughters, shooting them and leaving them to die in his taxicab in a suburb of Dallas. Amina, eighteen, and Sarah, seventeen, described by friends as extremely bright young girls, had become "westernized," creating conflict with their Muslim father who had migrated from Egypt in the 1980s. It was reported that Mr. Said was upset because the girls were involved in relationships with non-Muslims. He also was disturbed by the clothes his daughters were wearing and took matters into his own hands, taking both their lives.[16]

HONOR KILLINGS

Honor killings are commonplace in other democratic countries where Muslims are living.

Let's see what is happening in Europe.

Germany

Even in Germany, there have been many cases of honor killings. The murder of Hatin Surucu, who was twenty-three, is illustrative of the fact that the issue is primarily an Islamic one. Hatin was gunned down at the bus station by her three brothers. Investigators strongly suspect that it was an honor killing because her fundamentalist Turkish-Kurdish family strongly disapproved of her modern, un-Islamic lifestyle. Hatin had grown up in Berlin, but had married her cousin at the age of sixteen and moved to Istanbul. A few years later, she had returned to Berlin with her young son and had moved into a home for single mothers. She completed school and had begun training to become an electrician. Living like any other young German girl and abandoning her Islamic dress had eventually gotten her killed.[17]

Sweden

A Muslim father living in Sweden killed his daughter after she refused to marry the Turkish man of his choice. Rahmi killed his daughter, Fadime Sahindal, as she left the apartment where she had gone to secretly meet her mother and sister. Fadime had been in hiding because her father had previously threatened to kill her because she was dating a young Swedish boy.[18]

Australia

Even further afield in Australia, honor killings are occurring. Pela Atroshi, who was nineteen years old, was murdered in Iraq by the male head of her family. The killing had been masterminded by her grandfather, a Kurd living in Australia, and had also involved her father and his three brothers. A Kurdish Swede by citizenship, Pela was deceived into returning to Iraq, her homeland, for a vacation. Her family's frustration over her decision to leave Iraq again had led to her eventual death at the hands of her uncle, who shot her point blank in the head. The strong adherence of her family to restrictive Kurdish traditions had forced her sad honour killing.[19]

So what is the real Islam? Is Islam a religion of peace, as put forth by Muslim scholars who preach to the Western world, which gives meaning and hope to all who call upon the name of Allah? Would these victims of the violence perpetrated against them by adherents of Islam be able to say, "Islam means Peace," or would they tell a different story?

End Notes

1) www.mefact.com/cache/html/human-right/honor-killings:isitislam:Syed Karan Mirza, July 1, 2005.

2) http://www.islam-watch.org/SyedKamranMirza/honor_killing.htm

3) ibid.

4) ibid.

5) ibid.

6) www.stophonorkillings.com

7) www.wikiislam.net/wiki/images:violence-against-women

8) www.news.bbc.co.uk/2/hi/programmes/correspondence/909948.

9) www.sulivan-country-com-idu/cul death.9.

10) www.foxnews.com/story/0,2933,335,533

11) www.jihadwatch.org/2008/.../honor-killing-over-facebook-in-Saudi-Arabia-Cleric-vehemently-condemns-facebook, Posted at April 1, 2008.

12) www.independent.co.uk>news>world>Middle East.

13) www.persecution.net/so-2010=12=09.

15) www.humanevents.com/articles.php?id=30856.

16) www.foxnews.com/story/02933,377044.00.

17) Sonia Phalnikar, March 2005, DW-World. DE; Ext. Honor Killing Shocks Berlin.

18) The Seattle Time Company.

19) www.news.com.au/Australian-links-to-brutal-honor-killing/story.

Chapter **6**
The Mirage of After Life

Previously, we have discussed the reasons a woman becomes the subject of all kinds of abuse in the Muslim world and is basically considered a source of shame to her family. Even the words associated with women are demeaning or reduce them to their sexual function. Others reinforce the necessity for modesty and the shame that any infraction of Islamic codes of behavior by women will bring on the community. Muhammad proclaimed women "awrah," which translated means "object of shame." "Awrah" is defined in the *Encyclopaedia of Islam* as "pudendum or external genitals, especially belonging to a female."

In Pakistan, India, and Bangladesh, the word used for a woman is "auraate," which is derived from the Arabic word "awrah." It is usually used as a synonym for women as an expression of hatred and shame.

So where does this end for the shamed Muslim woman? Is it paradise or hell on earth for her? Any woman who still thinks and hopes that Islam will bring her freedom, liberty, equality, justice, and care for her emotional and physical well-being is merely fooling herself. Her "privilege" to enjoy her life right here on earth as gifted to her by her Allah is contingent on her ability to:

1. Produce as many children as she can.

2. Watch silently and passively as her husband brings as many as three other wives into the marriage (if he can afford them), as he long as he treats them all equally.

3. Marry the man her parents decide is best for her even if he is seventy years old.

4. Be divorced by her husband as he pleases.

5. Always be required to travel outside the home with an escort. When she goes outside, the devil welcomes her, so she must always be careful to stay at home or only go out with male protection.

6. Sustain abuse at her husband's hand, as he determines, verbally or by beatings.

If a woman fails to live within these confines and strays outside Islamic laws by being found in a pre-marital or extra-marital relationship, she puts herself in danger of being executed, usually by stoning.

Does she see anything wrong in the above behavior? She opens her eyes to a life built on cruel and unforgiving Islamic laws, never seeing the outside world for what it is. How could she distinguish? She hopelessly prays for her salvation and the slim chance of entering her final destination of Paradise. If she gets there, or if she is worthy of entering, that is also determined by Prophet Muhammad himself. Although the woman's fate is determined by Allah, it is evident from the Hadiths that Muhammad issues the woman's sentence. Many of the Hadiths concern themselves with the eternal fate of women and how few women are worthy of, or will indeed enter, Paradise. For example, in an interesting conversation, Muhammad reveals his view of women:

Once Allah's Apostle went out to the Musalla (to offer the prayers)—Id-al-Adha or Al-Fitr prayer. Then he passed by the women and said, "O women! Give alms, as I have seen that the majority of the dwellers of hell-fire were you (women)." They asked, "Why is it so, O Allah's Apostle?" He replied, "You curse frequently and are ungrateful to your husbands. I have not seen anyone more deficient in intelligence and religion than you. A cautious sensible man could be led astray by some of you." The women asked, "O Allah's Apostle! What is deficient in our intelligence and religion?" He said, "Is not the evidence of two women equal to the witness of one man?" They replied in the affirmative. He said, "This is the deficiency in her intelligence. Isn't it true that a woman can neither pray nor fast during her menses?" The women replied in the affirmative. He said, "This is the deficiency in her religion." Sahih Bukhari 1:6:301: Narrated Abu Said Al-Khudri

And, Muhammad continues to expresses his thought as: IUsama b Zaid reports:

"I stood at the door of paradise. I found that the overwhelming majority of those who entered therein was that of poor persons, and the wealthy persons were detained to get into that. The denizens of Hell were commanded to get into Hell. And I stood upon the door of fire, and the majority amongst them who entered there was that of women."

The horrifying fate of women is expressed even more clearly in the hadiths of Kanz al-'Ummal, 22:10:

> "Out of ninety-nine women, one is in Paradise, and the rest are in Hell."

He goes on the record that [Muhammad said]:

> "A believing woman is the same as a white-footed raven among the ravens. Fire has been created for the senseless, and women are the most senseless of all." Kanz al-'Ummal, 22:11

And a severe warning is given to women to be subservient in all things to their husbands:

> "The Prophet once said to a woman: 'Watch how you treat your husband, for he is your paradise and your hell.'" Kanz al-'Ummal, Vol. 22 Hadiths # No. 868

Other hadiths are explicit in their description of the fate of women:

> "In Hell, I saw women hanging by their breasts. They had fathered bastards." Ishaq: 185

The result of such teaching means that millions of Muslim women are in continual pursuit of pleasing their husbands while on earth so that they may be among the one percent who will enter Paradise according to their prophet. That hope keeps them enduring all the physical and mental abuse that they are subjected to. What they will receive in Paradise is another question. Will they be given the same worldly pleasures as have been promised to the Muslim men? Are they as lucky as their men and receive the same privileges that the men are going to receive, mainly WOMEN, WINE and WEALTH, as promised by Allah himself?

The faithful men who enter Paradise will receive houris (beautiful virgins) and fresh youths (boys) in Paradise that never age for their gratification. Surah 79:19 describes these divine promises. According to the Qur'an, the following will be bestowed on the faithful ones:

> "And give glad tidings to those who believe and do righteous good deeds that for them will be Gardens under which rivers flow (Paradise)... Whenever they are provided with a provision of fruit there-from, they will say, 'This is what we were provided with before.' And it is given to them in likeness. And they will have therein purified spouses and they will abide therein eternally." Qur'an 2:25

> "...they will sit with bashful, dark-eyed virgins, as chaste as the sheltered eggs of ostriches." Qur'an 37:40-48

Reinforcement of this promise is repeated in the Qur'an:

> "We created the houris and made them virgins, loving companions for those on the right hand..." Qur'an 56:34-37

The Hadiths further proclaim the abundance of houris in Paradise, as evidenced in the following verses where an enthralling picture is painted:

"Every man who enters Paradise shall be given seventy-two houris; no matter at what age he died, when he is admitted into Paradise, he will become a thirty year old and shall not age any further. A man in Paradise shall be given virility equal to that of one hundred men." Al-Tirmizi, Vol. 2, pg. 138

The portrait of these apparitions demonstrates the mind of Allah himself:

"A houri is a most beautiful young woman with a transparent body. The marrow of her bones is visible like the interior of pearls and rubies. She looks like wine in a white glass. She is of white color and free from the routine physical disabilities of an ordinary woman, such as menstruation, menopause, urinal and offal discharge, child-bearing, and the related pollution. A houri is a girl of a tender age, having large breasts, which are round (pointed) and not inclined to dangle. Houris dwell in palaces of splendid surroundings." Al-Tirmizi, Vol. 2, pgs. 35-40

Houris are always the main topic of conversation for the afterlife, but that is not all that these dedicated followers of the prophet will be gaining when they arrive in Paradise. Additionally, they will be granted all the worldly possessions that they had wished for while on earth.

Paradise is an essentially materialistic place, where rich rewards of jewels, sumptuous food, and luxuries are given to the faithful. It is a place of indulgence and indolence, a place where all physical appetites are catered for. The

Qur'an is explicit in enumerating the pleasures to come for the faithful ones:

> "As for those who have faith and who do good work, God will admit them to gardens watered by running streams. They shall be decked with pearls and bracelets of gold, and arrayed in garments of silk." Qur'an 22:23

The promise of the Qur'an is that of plenty, filled with earthly, sensual, and erotic pleasures, the desire for which not many human beings (made of soil) can withstand.

> "Enter ye the Garden, Ye and your wives, in beauty and rejoicing. To them will be passed round dishes and goblets of gold; there will be there all that the soul could desire, all that the eyes could delight in; and ye shall abide there..."
> Qur'an 43:68-73

The entrance into Paradise is only through good works as Qur'an 3:136 shows:

> "These shall be rewarded with forgiveness from their Lord and with gardens watered by running streams, where they shall dwell forever. Blessed is the reward of those who do good works."

And the Qur'an mentions the abundance awaiting the faithful:

> "In them will be Two Springs pouring forth water in continuous abundance; then which of

the favours of your Lord will you deny?" Qur'an
55:66-67

WINE will also flow in abundance in Paradise according
to these verses:

> "Here is the Parable of the Garden which the righ-
> teous are promised. In it are...rivers of wine..."
> Qur'an 47:15

Nothing could be further from the truth than this ridicu-
lous claim of the Qur'an:

> "But the true servants of God shall be well pro-
> vided for...they shall be served with goblets filled
> at a gushing fountain, white and delicious to those
> who drink it. It will neither dull their senses nor
> befuddle them." Qur'an 37:40-48

> "The righteous will surely dwell in bliss. Reclin-
> ing upon soft couches, they will gaze around
> them: and in their faces you shall mark the glow
> of joy. They shall be given a pure wine to drink,
> securely sealed, whose very dregs are mush..."
> Qur'an 83:23-26

The FOODS in Paradise will consist of eternal fruits, as
evidenced by the following verses:

> "This is the Paradise which the righteous have
> been promised...eternal are its fruits, and eternal
> are its shades..." Qur'an 13:35

"Here is a Parable of the Garden which the righteous are promised: ...In it are rivers of milk of which the taste never changes; rivers of wine, a joy to those who drink; and rivers of honey pure and clear. In it there are for them all kinds of fruits; and grace from their Lord..." Qur'an 47:15

Many times in the Institute which I attended, during Islamic studies class, which we all had to attend, the concept of Paradise was explained to the young students. Although the explicitly graphic sexual details were not discussed, one point was always stressed, and that was the abundance of the food and fruits that on earth the student always desired to eat. When asked their opinion about Paradise, they would be so excited to share their innocent views. One particular student, who was five years old, told me that his teacher had described to them how many sweets they could eat in Paradise. He could not wait to eat the abundant supply of fruits, chocolates, candies, and ice cream. The way Paradise was pictured to the children sounded to me more like the movie *Charlie and the Chocolate Factory*.

Indeed "Paradise" sounds like an enticing place to go. This picture of Paradise has its origins in the longings of those living in the harsh environment of the Northern Arabian desert, which was dry and very hostile at the time of Muhammad. Even though along the coast the South receives regular rainfall and has had abundant plant life, the North East is still especially inhospitable with little water and little plant life, except for the date palm. Due to its extreme and harsh environment, this area has been inhabited by Bedouin Arabs, who are nomadic shepherds who have lived in small tribal groups for most of their history. In the Bedouin Arab society, women were dehumanized, and child marriage and female infanticide were common. With life as an on-going struggle against the forces of nature, comprised of desert storms and a harsh environment, the mental make-up of the Bedouin Arabs has been shaped by the mindset of kill or be killed.[1]

Muhammad understood the mindset of the people he lived with very well. To gain their favour so that they would follow him, he tempted them with the promise of eternal pleasures of the things they were lusting for on earth. He needed to entice the Arabs to unite and fight his enemies, the pagans and the Jews. In the hopes of receiving their eternal reward, they became fearless fighters for the afterlife. This was the key factor that brought Muhammad victory after victory over the Arab Pagans. It is for this reason that even today, 1.7 billion human beings are not only subdued, but also anxious and obedient to their faith. They are in a hurry to escape hellfire and go directly to Paradise to receive their rewards.[2]

The Islamic hope of salvation is measured on a sliding scale. To attain their salvation, a Muslim must focus his life on the five pillars of Islam:

1. **Shahada**: "There is no God but Allah, and Muhammad is the Prophet of Allah."

2. **Prayer**: It must be performed five times a day in Arabic while facing Mecca, the Holy City.

3. **Giving Alms (Zakat)**: It is the obligatory duty to give 2.5 percent of one's total income to help others.

4. **Fasting**: Muslims are supposed to fast during the entire month of Ramadan. The fasting lasts from

sunrise to sunset and is considered atonement for their sins over the previous year.

5. **Pilgrimage to Mecca**: This travel to the Holy City should be achieved at least once in a Muslim's life. A woman must be accompanied by a male Muslim.

Additionally, joining in "JIHAD" is a sure visa to Paradise. *Front Page Magazine* reports the remarks of a proud mother who sacrificed her three sons for the sake of Allah. In her statements before and after the suicidal attack of one of her sons in 2002, she said:

> "By Allah, today is the best day of my life. I feel that our lord is pleased with me because I am offering something (my son) for him. I wish to sacrifice more sons for Allah's forgiveness and for the flag of Islam... it's true that there is nothing more precious than children, but for the sake of Allah, what is precious becomes cheap." At the end of her statement she says, "What more can I ask for? Allah willing, the lord will promise us Paradise; that's the best I can hope for. The greatest honor (my son) showed me is his martyrdom."[3]

Which mother in her right mind would want to sacrifice her children for a paradise that does not promise her anything! No matter what, Muslims try their best to make Allah happy, thus continuing to perform good deeds, for they believe that their passport to salvation is by good works. If a Muslim's good works outnumber his bad ones, and if Allah so wills it, he may be forgiven all his indiscretions and enter into Paradise. Consider the following verses from the Qur'an:

"To those who believe and do deeds of righteousness hath Allah promised forgiveness and a great reward." Qur'an 5:9

"O you who believe! If you are careful of (your duty to) Allah, He will grant you a distinction and do away with your evils and forgive you; and Allah is the Lord of mighty grace." Qur'an 8:29

And again we read:

"Then those whose balance (of good deeds) is heavy, they will be successful. But those, whose balance is light, will be those who have lost their souls; in hell will they abide." Qur'an 23:102-103

The hope for entry into Paradise for a Muslim depends on good works, rather than on grace. The anxiety produced by wondering if your good deeds outweigh your bad deeds is burdensome to many Muslims. The peace of a Christian, who knows that everything for salvation has been accomplished by the Lord Jesus Christ in His atoning death, is in stark contrast to the stress experienced by Muslims, who continually perform rites and defend the honour of Islam, sometimes with violence and at great cost to women especially. As believers, we know that we are saved by God's grace through our faith in Jesus Christ. Our comfort lies in the fact that:

"For by grace are ye saved through faith; and that not yourselves: it is the gift of God: Not of works, lest any man should boast." Ephesians 2:8-9

This assurance is that we are justified not by works, but by the faith of Christ:

> "Knowing that a man is not justified by the works of the law, but by the faith of Jesus Christ, even we have believed in Jesus Christ, that we might be justified by the faith of Christ, and not by the works of the law: for by the works of the law shall no flesh be justified." Galatians 2:16

The only way we can be exalted in God's eyes is through His Son Jesus Christ, who shed His blood for us.

When I was working, I noted that many of my male Muslim colleagues would often have a black mark on their foreheads caused by constantly bowing down during prayers and touching their foreheads to the ground. This mark represented how dedicated to prayer they were, practicing this ritual five times a day, three hundred and sixty-five days a year. They always fasted thirty days during Ramadan and gave the prescribed alms. Yet many were unable to complete the pilgrimage to Mecca in Saudi Arabia due to the expense. These Muslims were never sure whether they had any hope of entering Paradise, for they had not completed one of the five pillars set out to attain salvation.

The Muslims' uncertainty was also based on the uncertainty of their Prophet Muhammad, for he could offer no assurance of salvation for himself either. You may have encountered a Muslim's use of the phrase, "Peace be upon him," when speaking Muhammad's name. Does that mean that 1.7 billion Muslims today still believe that Muhammad is not at peace with Allah? Even though they believe Muhammad is the Perfect Man, no-one can be sure of his fate.

In the following verses, it is clear that Muhammad himself feared for his afterlife and worried about the uncertainty of his salvation:

> "Or do they say, 'He has forged it? Say: If I have forged it, you have no power to help me against Allah. He knows very well what you are pressing upon; He suffices as a witness between me and you; He is the all-forgiving, the all-compassionate. Say: 'I am not an innovation among the messengers, and I know not what shall be done with me or with you. I only follow what is revealed to me; I am only a clear Warner (sic warning)." Qur'an 46:8-9

The next verse also highlights that Muhammad knew that he was not capable of assuring others about their salvation.

> When Allah revealed the Verse: "Warn your nearest kinsmen," Allah's Apostle got up and said, "O people of Quraish (or said similar words)! Buy (i.e. save) yourselves (from the Hellfire) as I cannot save you from Allah's Punishment; O Bani Abd Manaf! I cannot save you from Allah's Punishment, O Safiya, the Aunt of Allah's Apostle! I cannot save you from Allah's Punishment; O Fatima bint Muhammad! Ask me anything from my wealth, but I cannot save you from Allah's Punishment." Narrated Abu Huraira:Sahih al-Bakhari, Vol. 4, Book 51, No. 16.

Muhammad was apparently telling the truth. How could he give a guarantee and hope to others about their eternity when he himself was powerless and hopeless according to the writings of the Hadith? Why was Muhammad so worried about his salvation? This is what people must understand, when Muhammad's own salvation depends on your praying for all eternity, seeking salvation through him is simply foolish, isn't it?

Muhammad claimed himself to be a messenger of Allah, yet his actions proved him to be ungodly.[4] Fighting seventy-four battles, all of which except one were offensive. Killing, torturing, raping, and enslaving victims, as well as lusting for women, are definitely not godly behavior. The Hadiths are full of his recorded history, which makes grim reading—and is hardly an example that should be followed.

Muslims all over the world are so blinded by this "Prince of Darkness" that it seems they are unable to understand what Muslim teachings really mean. They are strictly prohibited from questioning the authority of the Qur'an.

> "O ye who believe! Ask not questions about things which if made plain to you, may cause you trouble. Some people before you did ask such questions, and on that account lost their faith." Sura 5:101-10.

This blind faith is due to the constant fear of going to Hell, because Allah has commanded them not to question his authority, and disobeying this command will open the doors of Hell for them. The use of the word "Hell" exists over two hundred times in the Qur'an, followed by "Day of Judgment," which is repeated 163 times, and "Resurrection," which is written 117 times. So Muslims believe in resurrection, in judgement, and in Hell, and the result for them is fear and no assurance.

Allah, who will be judging all people, is a very distant god who wishes no relationship with his people. This principle of judgment has caused great fear in the hearts of Muslims.

> "If Allah so willed, He could make you all one people: But He leads astray whom He pleases and guides whom He pleases, but ye shall certainly be called to account for all your actions."
> Qur'an 16:93

This means that if you sin, Allah must have led you to do it. Yet he will throw you into Hell when you die![5]

The following verses from the Qur'an may give a clearer picture of the intentions of Allah for those who have hope:

> "The unbelievers say, 'Why is not a sign sent down to him from his Lord?' Say, 'Truly Allah leaveth, to stray, whom he will; But he guideth to himself those who turn to him in penitence.'"
> Qur'an 13:27

The problem is that being able to pass this test of faith and to gain admittance to Paradise is not in our hand.

> "Now Allah leaves straying to those whom he pleases and guides whom he pleases; and he exalted in power, full of wisdom." Qur'an 14:4

Since God is omnipotent, this means that no one can guide anyone whom Allah misleads, because no one is capable of counteracting Allah's actions. This fact is confirmed by Al-Nisa 4:89 and 4:143—

> "They but wish that ye should reject Faith, as they do, and thus be on the same footing (as they); But take not friends from their ranks until they flee in the way of Allah (from what is forbidden). But if they turn renegades, seize them and slay them whenever ye find them; and (in any case) take no friends or helpers from their rank." Qur'an 4:89

For me, it is confusing to understand why a god who is able to guide people chooses to lead them astray and then fills Hell with those whom he himself has misled.

> "(They are) distracted in mind even in the midst of it, being (sincerely) for neither one group nor for another whom Allah leaves straying—never wilt thou find for him the way." Qur'an 4:143

When Muslim authorities are questioned regarding the hope of salvation for men and women, or any other issue in the Qur'an, you will notice that their answers will never be direct. They will tend to evade the issue. If you wish to question them, please be warned. They will use deception in order to maintain a positive image of Islam in the eyes of the Westerner. That is a main reason why so many people are attracted to Islam; they hear only what the Muslims want them to hear.

Muslims are constantly looking for an opportunity to invite non-believers to discuss the benefits of conversion to

Islam. They present a vivid picture of what a glorious life will be given to the believers when they leave this world.

One such example took place when a colleague of mine, Saima, extended an invitation to me to discuss the Muslim faith. She was one of the women in my workplace who hated Christians and attempted to misinterpret the Bible, always seeking an opportunity to discredit non-Muslims. Her tactic included trying to aggravate her non-Muslim colleagues so they would use harsh words against Islam and be accused of blasphemy.

One day, Saima approached me and asked point blank, "Sarah, why don't you accept Islam? You know you will be a very lucky and blessed woman."

I took a deep breath and smiled at her and said, "Thank you, Saima. I appreciate it. Will it be ok if when you have some time you could help me to clarify my questions?" I noticed a sparkle in her eyes as she walked passed me. I knew that she would now take time out to attempt to evangelize and convince me to convert to Islam.

Later that day, we met in a corner of the cafeteria. She began quoting verses from the Qur'an and the Hadiths and elaborating on how a woman is respected in Islam. She pointed out how Muhammad respected his wives and treated them equally. Anyone not well versed in the Qur'an and Hadiths could have easily been misled, as Saima was very convincing indeed. I knew that she was not going to give up easily, and I was beginning to feel that her attempt to convert me was becoming hard to endure. Though I seemed attentive, I was praying silently and seeking God's wisdom and words to let her know that no one could take the place of Jesus Christ in my life and heart.

Finally I said, "Saima, thank you for sharing your knowledge of Islam with me; I get your point. However, I am still not clear on one most important issue. The Qur'an and Hadith talk at great length about the afterlife of a man. In Paradise, the faithful one (a man) will get rewards of seventy-two virgins and honey and exotic fruits. Why is it that these rewards are only for MEN? What will the women get in this Paradise? Do they have hope of any rewards? What hope and assurance do you personally have to enter Paradise?"

Saima's facial expression now changed. Her face turned red, and her lips suddenly became dry. Her voice became higher than before, perhaps showing her attempt to intimidate me, and she stammered as she searched for an explanation to hide her embarrassment and confusion. Finally she said, "I know there is an answer to it. I just have to ask my Mulana Ji (Islamic Clergyman) and then let you know."

I took her hand in my hand and warmly proclaimed, "Saima, if I die this second, I have complete assurance and hope that I will be with my living Saviour in Heaven. I do not have to worry about searching for the answers because I know that Christ has saved me and that I am assured of my salvation. He did it through His ultimate personal sacrifice. There is no shadow of a doubt, and nothing can change that truth."

She nodded her head and left.

Muslims have built their faith on many unreliable practices and beliefs. They have no assurance of salvation, and the Paradise they are promised—if they are judged worthy to enter—is one of physical enjoyment for men, as they receive riches, wonderful food, and sex with many virgins. And for the women—the few women who make it to Paradise— what? We know for certain that Christ is the only hope; we do not have to struggle to please God. We know that everything to enable men and women to enter into Heaven has already been done on the Cross. We have complete assurance because of His promises and because of the Lord Jesus Christ who died and rose again so that all who believe in Him will not perish but will have eternal life.

End Notes

1) wikiislam.net/wiki/Islam.

2) www.Australian-Islamist Monitor/islammonitor.org/Islamic Heaven.

3) www.frontmagazine.com/.../fatah-praise-proud-mother. Al-Hayat, Al-Jidida March 18, 2013.

4) www.answering-islam.org/authors. .Mohammad_salvation/article written by Sam Shamoun, "Was Mohammah certain of his salvation?"

5) G.J.O Moshay, "Who is this Allah?" Pg 98, Paragraph 3.

Chapter 7
The Assurance

THE GREATEST ACT

As a Christian, we can be confident in our belief of how we are saved and where we will be after our death. Our relationship with God and the rewards of Heaven are guaranteed in the Bible, since it is based on Jesus' finished work on the Cross. He paid the ultimate price for our sins. Our God is the God of Love, whose love for us in not based on merit, but on His infinite nature. He shows us this nature in poignant verses from the Bible:

> "For God so loved the world that He gave His only begotten Son, that whosoever believeth in Him should not perish, but have everlasting life." John 3:16

> "But God commendeth His love toward us, in that, while we were yet sinners, Christ died for us." Romans 5:8

Our God of the Bible does not love us because we are good. He loves us despite our sins, and therefore, He made a provision to save us from those sins and forgive us of the ones that we have committed.

> "We love Him, because He first loved us." 1 John 4:19

The plan of our salvation has existed from the beginning. In His mercy, He has revealed His qualities to us. God is Spirit—by nature intangible.

> "God is a Spirit: and they that worship Him must worship Him in spirit and in truth." John 4:24

God is one, but He exists as three Persons: God the Father, the Son, and the Holy Spirit.

> "And Jesus, when He was baptized, went up straightway out of the water: and, lo, the heavens were opened unto Him, and He saw the Spirit of God descending like a dove, and lighting upon Him. And lo a voice from heaven, saying, This is My beloved Son, in whom I am well pleased." Matthew 3:16-17

He is unchanging:

> "For I am the Lord, I change not; therefore ye sons of Jacob are not consumed." Malachi 3:6

He is Omnipresent—everywhere:

> "Whither shall I go from Thy spirit? or whither shall I flee from Thy presence? If I ascend up into heaven, Thou art there: if I make my bed in hell, behold, Thou art there. If I take the wings of the morning, and dwell in the uttermost parts of the sea; Even there shall Thy hand lead me, and Thy right hand shall hold me." Psalm 139:7-12

He is Incomparable:

> "Wherefore Thou art great, O Lord God: for there
> is none like Thee, neither is there any God beside
> Thee, according to all that we have heard with our
> ears." 2 Samuel 7:22

God created the world and has compassion for it. His love is not only for Christians, but for all the people of the world. He is executing His eternal plan (Ephesians 1:11), which involves the redemption of man from the curse of sin and death (Galatians 3:13-14).

We here on earth have a relationship with Him, because the Son of God became the Son of Man and is therefore the "bridge" between God and man (John 14:6; 1 Timothy 2:5). It is only through the Son that we can receive forgiveness for our sins (Ephesians 1:7), reconciliation with God (John 15:15; Romans 5:10), and eternal salvation (2 Timothy 2:10). In Jesus Christ, "all the fullness of the Deity lives in bodily form" (Colossians 2:9). So, to have a relationship with God, we need to know and believe Jesus.[1]

He demonstrates His Unconditional Love.

The Gospel message is basically a story of divine rescue. God is determined to save us from our sins, and it is based on His unconditional love (Ephesians 1:4-5). Christ willingly offered Himself as a Compensation for our sins, and this rescue mission results in a gracious act of self-sacrifice (John 15:13).

Jesus' compassion for the world is demonstrated in the following verse:

"For God sent not His Son into the world to condemn the world; but that the world through Him might be saved." John 3:17

The Apostle John tells us:

"That ye might believe that Jesus is the Christ, the Son of God; and that ye might have life through His name." John 20:31

Believing Jesus means believing in His name; and His name means Jehovah our Salvation or our Savior.

And the Apostle Paul teaches us:

"That if thou shalt confess with thy mouth the Lord Jesus, and shalt believe in thine heart that God hath raised Him from the dead, thou shalt be saved. For with the heart man believeth unto righteousness; and with the mouth confession is made unto salvation. For the Scripture saith, Whosoever believeth on Him shall not be ashamed." Romans 10: 9-11

What a wonderful confidence we have knowing that we are forgiven because of the shedding of the blood of Jesus. And then the Apostle John further confirms:

"But as many as received Him, to them gave He power to become the sons of God, even to them that believe on His name." John 1:12

God becomes our Father, and we are His children. We can say for certain that Biblical Christianity offers Heaven to whoever believes in the Lord Jesus Christ and abides in Him. It is not because of our good works, as we have none to offer, but is because the sacrifice of Jesus Christ covers it all. The Bible clearly gives assurance to Christians in these comforting words:

> "These things have I written unto you that believe on the name of the Son of God; that ye may know that ye have eternal life, and that ye may believe on the name of the Son of God." 1 John 5:13

These powerful words give me sound confidence that my name is written in the Book of Life, just as the Lord Jesus said to Martha, a woman:

> "I am the Resurrection, and the Life: he that believeth in Me, though he were dead, yet shall he live." John 11:25

How different this is from the fear and anxiety felt by Muslims who do not know what their ultimate fate will be.

THE HEAVEN OF THE BIBLE IS ALL ABOUT GOD

When the Bible speaks of Heaven, we are assured of being in the presence of the Lord. There will be no death, sadness, or pain. We will worship and praise our Lord, and He will be our constant delight and satisfaction. The focus will be on Him. In contrast with the Muslim emphasis on sexual pleasure, Luke 20:28-35 states that there will be no physical marriage in Heaven as there is on earth. Physical relationships will not hold the same importance as they do here on earth.

How different is Heaven from Paradise, where Islam promotes sex and other fleshly desires. Muslim men hope they will eat fruits they have never eaten before and will never become intoxicated with wine and will enjoy indulging in an abundance of sexual pleasures.

In contrast, the joy of the Christian Heaven is not in drinking and in lustful desires, but rather in righteousness, peace, and joy in the Holy Spirit. Heaven is where God is, and where God is, it is Holy and perfect. Heaven, which is His dwelling place, is holy and perfect. It is where all—men and women—who believe in Him as His people will live in the light of His presence and where there will be no more tears and no more pain. Death will be no more.

In the Psalms, we read that God Himself is our home:

"A Father of the fatherless, and a Judge of the widows, is God in His holy habitation." Psalm 68:5

The New Testament focuses on the purpose of Heaven more than telling us what it is like or where it is. We read, on the other hand, that Hell is for separation and punishment:

"But the children of the kingdom shall be cast out into outer darkness: there shall be weeping and gnashing of teeth." Matthew 8:12

Heaven, however, is for fellowship and eternal joy and, more importantly, worshipping around the throne of God.[2]

My heart pours out to the Muslims, and I pray that they will someday come to know who Jesus Christ is. I also believe that they are blinded by the spirit of darkness and cannot discern between truth and lies. As believers, we know that Christ makes no distinction between a man and a woman as far as salvation is concerned; He views them as equal in the sight of God. Just as Christ met the Samaritan woman at the well, so also does He meet everyone—man or woman—at the Cross. He calls us His SONS and DAUGHTERS. Note the powerful verses proclaiming this equality:

> "But before faith came, we were kept under the law, shut up unto the faith which should afterwards be revealed. Wherefore the law was our schoolmaster to bring us unto Christ, that we might be justified by faith. But after that faith is come, we are no longer under a schoolmaster. For ye are all the children of God by faith in Christ Jesus. For as many of you as have been baptized into Christ have put on Christ. There is neither Jew nor Greek, there is neither bond nor free, there is neither male nor female: for ye are all one in Christ Jesus. And if ye be Christ's, then are ye Abraham's seed, and heirs according to the promise." Galatians 3:23-29

If you have ever visited a Muslim country, you have most likely heard the Islamic prayers recited through loud speakers from a nearby Mosque five times a day. After spending most of my life in the Middle East, I can still hear the prayers ringing in my ears—the same words repeated over and over again each day. To me, it always sounded as if they were merely reciting words without emotion. As far as Ramadan was concerned, almost all of my colleagues would fast, except the women who were experiencing their menstrual cycles or some illness. However, the amazing thing to me was that, whether they fasted or not, all pretended to be observing Ramadan and would openly announce it to all.

Only a few of my colleagues were able to travel to Mecca to perform Hajj (the pilgrimage to Mecca). Those who returned were accorded great respect and considered to be pious, bringing back Abe Zamzam (holy water), dates, and bracelets engraved with the name of Muhammad. These mementoes were then distributed among families and friends. One of my colleagues, Adnan, returned from Mecca in 2005, bringing me a bracelet and asking me to wear it.

He said, "Please accept the bracelet with Prophet Muhammad's name, and he will bless you." This was yet another challenge for me as a Christian living in a Muslim world.

I replied, "Adnan, I respect you, and you are a good friend of mine. But please do not ask me to wear this bracelet. You know that I will not, but I can give it to my neighbors who are also Muslim. I know that they will appreciate it more than words. I hope you don't mind."

Yet, another act that I saw Muslims performing was giving alms. They gave not only the set percentage as required by Islamic law, but they would give extra to the poor. If an outsider had an opportunity to witness this giving, it might appear very generous and appealing. However, these acts are performed only to please Allah. This they call Sadaqa, which involves voluntary charitable work. It may be given to the poor in form of money or sacrificing an animal. In my home country, I had seen this very often, specially to bring blessings to an occasion like a wedding, personal success, the birth of a child, or instances of sadness. Sadaqa is often performed to ward off evil.[3]

In the eight month of my second pregnancy, a couple of my colleagues were very inquisitive to know the sex of the child. However, I revealed this mystery to them one week before my due date. When they heard that the child was a boy, they advised me to give Sadaqa by slaughtering or sacrificing a black goat for the sake of Allah and distribute the meat to the poor. I thought to myself, "Now why in the world would I do that?" Well, they had solid reasons: firstly, to give thanks that I had been blessed with a male child, and secondly, to protect the child from evil eye. To this, I had only one comment to make to them:

> "Thank you for your advice, but my God who has formed this child in my womb has already placed His hedge of protection around him."

How blessed we are to have the joy of the Lord in our hearts. We need not worry about waking up daily and continually performing required religious duties in order to please God. But do not misunderstand the message here: we still need to spend time with God to hear His words and to share our hearts. However, we are under no law but to live with His grace. We do not have to live with the fear that, if we do not please God with our performance, He will punish us in eternal life. If we repent, He has promised that He will freely forgive us.

> "And they sung a new song, saying, Thou art worthy to take the book, and to open the seals thereof: for Thou wast slain, and hast redeemed us to God by Thy blood out of every kindred, and tongue, and people, and nation;" Revelation 5:9

It is God's desire that people of all nations know Him personally and be saved. Christ shares His heart when He says:

> "And He said unto me, It is done. I am Alpha and Omega, the beginning and the end. I will give unto him that is athirst of the fountain of the water of life freely." Revelation 21:6

I pray that numerous people in other nations will awaken and thirst for the salvation that Christ so lovingly offers to them.

End Notes

1) "Who is this Allah?" By G.J.O. Moshay, Chapter 5: Allah and The Sonship of Jesus, Pg-77.

2) www.gotquestions.org/where-is-Heaven.html.

3) www.islamwatch.org/.../1481-sadaqa-islamic-charity-for-the-poor.

Chapter 8
The Covenant

In the Muslim world, it is the parents' obligation and burden to obtain spouses for their children, especially their daughters. It is the head of the family, be it the father, grandfather, or uncle, who selects the future partner. This tradition still exists today in Middle Eastern countries, as well as in Southern Asia, Africa, and, in some cases, in Europe. It is implemented more strictly in the case of a female because the older males in the family are her guardians, and she is their responsibility. Thus, the decision is made on her behalf, oftentimes without her consent. Numerous factors determine her marriage eligibility: her family name, her family fortune, her beauty and lack of deformities, her education (to some extent), and how she maintains her home.

When my sisters and I were in our teens, our parents often reminded us that soon it would be time for us to get married. Respectful of our culture, even though our family was Christian, we knew that it would be our father who would choose our husbands; of course, our mother's consent was highly valued in this matter. I still remember that, when we would gather for any church event or even weddings, our mother would keep a sharp eye on the three of us. She would often remark, "Don't do anything crazy; I have the eyes of a tiger!"

We knew that she meant that we were not to become entangled with any man.

Today, as I look back, I appreciate the fact that our parents guided us on how to live a godly life. They both taught us many good things, reminding us that we should never get entrapped by deceiving men. For this reason, we kept ourselves at a distance from our Muslim male colleagues. My maternal grandfather always reminded my mother that "the worst Christian is a thousand times better than the best Muslim!"

At that time, we could not understand the wisdom of this statement, but with the passage of time, we came to realize what he had meant. My family had witnessed innumerable numbers of cases where Christian women, who had married Muslim men, later found that they were the second or third wife or were subjected to abusive treatment by husbands and/or in-laws—or sometimes were even sold into slavery.

Working in a professional environment, Muslim men would often attempt to flirt with us and draw us in with their charms. However, the careful advice of our parents ensured that they were picking the wrong targets. Knowing that we were Christians, we felt that they could never be sincere toward infidels such as we were in their eyes. The repeated reminders of the cruel episodes that we had witnessed of Christian/Muslim marriages made us even more conscious of the dangers that surrounded us.

My younger sister, who loves the Lord, has a remarkable testimony herself. She is a very pretty woman. In her college and career life, many young Muslim and Hindu men proposed to her. They were very good looking, career-oriented, and wealthy. They often showered her with flowers, chocolate, cards, and other expensive gifts. However, these things were usually returned. Her close friends, who envied her, told her that she was very foolish to miss the golden opportunity. However, she always told them, "Men and wealth come and go, but I cannot afford to lose my Christ. He carried the cross for my shame and set me free from my sins—an act of such sacrifice—and you want me to deny Him just to get worldly pleasures from ones who deny His existence!" To accept the gifts was to accept the men's beliefs and compromise on the deity of Christ. She often finished her conversation with a funny note: "Here, you can have them; enjoy it while it lasts." She still continues to wait for the life partner whom she strongly believes is arranged by God.

I am unable to speak for all couples, but I do know that the majority of Christian women, who have married a true believer of Jesus Christ, are very happy in their marriages. I feel strongly that it is Christ who makes the Christian marriage so beautiful and strong, and if He is taken out of our married life, then surely our marriage will never be what it was intended to be. He teaches us to be patient, forgiving, loving, and compromising. Marriage is designed by God, as we see in Gen. 2:22-24, and He has already prepared our partners before we even realize it. He has said: "It is not good for a man to be alone. Hence I will provide a helpmate for him, and they no longer will be two, but one flesh." A woman is no less than a man. God never instructed that they are either inferior or superior to each other because both are made in His image. The marriage between a man and a woman is a spiritual example between Christ and the church. Christ gave himself for the church, and He loves honors and protects her as His "bride" (Rev.19:7-9).

My marriage to my husband was arranged by my parents. I had previously known my husband because we were family friends. This marriage was in no way imposed on me, but I was honored that my mother asked my consent in this important matter. My father had prayed to the Lord before the decision was made.

God knew that this man was the one for me and brought us together in April of 2000. The day I walked down the aisle, I was excited, yet full of questions. I thought, "Fine! I am about to say 'til death do us part,' but will this really work? Will he be able to understand and love me? Will I be able to be his good helpmate? What if he is abusive; will I suffer?" That is not to say that our marriage has been a fairy tale. Occasionally, we do have disagreements, but our love in the Lord has been the foundation of our life together. We are able to forgive each other and put the other first.

This love that we express is possible when Christ lives in us. The first and most important point is to be obedient to God and to His word and to remember that, with God in our marriage, all things are possible. How many times when we are experiencing marital conflicts do we sit together and pray about it? Many times our anger and egos get in the way, but with prayer, we are able to push them aside and realize the true feelings we have for each other through God. Ephesians 5:22-33 beautifully describes the relationship between a husband and a wife and how they are to treat one another. That relationship should be one of mutual dependence; they complement each other, existing together, not standing alone.

One day while I was having tea with my colleagues in the staff room, a very interesting conversation began. One of my co-workers, Habiba, was heartbroken because her husband was bringing home a third wife, a much younger one. She could not understand that. Why was her husband's appetite for women not fulfilled? Habiba felt jealous of the new wife.

Saima, whom I talked about earlier, was always excited to step in to promote the cause of Islam. To console her, she related the honorable life of her prophet and how he treated all his wives equally. She advised Habiba that she should be proud that her husband was following the footsteps of the holy prophet, and if she complained, she would not be honored by Allah. Noticing my presence, Saima turned to me," What do you think about it?" I knew her motive, and that was to get me into trouble if I condemned Muhammad's practice. In my heart, I asked the Holy Spirit to give me wisdom and, as always, He was there to rescue me.

"Saima," I said, "You believe that Allah created Adam, and out of his rib, he made Eve. You also believe that God—who, for you, is Allah—is almighty and has the power to do whatever he desires as the whole universe is in his hands."

"Yes, absolutely. It is written in the Qur'an," she said.

I replied, "Then, because you agree with me about Adam and Eve, here is a question to you. In the beginning when God made Adam, why did He take only one rib to make only one woman? He is Almighty. He could have given Adam a choice. But why only one?"

All of them looked spellbound, as this story is in the Qur'an, and questioning it meant trouble for them. They saw that in the beginning God intended there to be one man and one woman.

For the past five years, I have shared in churches and with the Christian community in the USA on various sensitive issues in the Islamic community: the role of women, the polygamous Muslim male, and the abuse of wives. Several women, who heard my lectures and who sadly did not have good marriages, but were being abused, came forward to question the Bible along with the Qur'an. One of the common questions in many cases was, "You talk about Muhammad being polygamous. How about in the Old Testament?" It is true that many of the Old Testament kings, including David and, of course, Solomon had more than one wife, as did the patriarchs, Abraham and Jacob. For most of the Old Testament period, it was culturally acceptable for men to enter into polygamous marriages.

The Bible, however, never endorses polygamy as in the command or purpose of God, and many women of the Bible suffered bitterness of heart because of their situation of being one wife amongst others. Hannah, for example, who eventually became the mother of Samuel, was taunted for her childlessness by her 'rival' so much so that she became very depressed and distressed. To find the perfect answer to this ambiguity, I turned to one good resource to help. An article in GotQuestions.org explains it all very well.

POLYGAMY AND MONOGAMY IN THE BIBLE

The question of polygamy is an interesting one. Why did God allow it in the Bible? The first recorded polygamy in the Bible was that of Lamech in Gen 4:19, who married two women. Due to patriarchal societies in the Old Testament, it was nearly impossible for an unmarried woman to provide for herself. A man would take multiple wives and served as a provider and protector of all of them. This protected the woman from being subjected to prostitution and slavery.

The next question is how does God view polygamy today? Even allowing polygamy, the Bible presents monogamy as the plan that conforms most closely to God's ideal for marriage. The Bible says that God's intention was for one man to be married to only one woman. "For this reason a man will leave his father and mother and be united to his wife [singular], and they will become one flesh [singular]" Gen 2:24.

In the New Testament, both 1 Tim 3:2, 12 and Titus 1:6 identify "the husband of one wife" in a list of qualifications for spiritual leadership. The phrase could literally be translated "a one-woman man." In no sense is a polygamist considered a one-woman man. Speaking of the relationship between husbands and wives, when referring to a husband (singular), it always refers to a wife (singular).

> "Wives, submit yourselves unto your own husbands, as unto the Lord. For the husband is the head of the wife, even as Christ is the Head of the church: and He is the Savior of the body. Therefore as the church is subject unto Christ, so let the wives be to their own husbands in everything. Husbands, love your wives, even as Christ also loved the church, and gave Himself for it; That He might sanctify and cleanse it with the washing of water by the word, That He might present it to Himself a glorious church, not having spot, or wrinkle, or any such thing; but that it should be holy and without blemish. So ought men to love their wives as their own bodies. He that loveth his wife loveth himself. For no man ever yet hated his own flesh; but nourisheth and cherisheth it, even as the Lord the church: For we are members of His body, of His flesh, and of His bones. For this cause shall a man leave his father and mother,

and shall be joined unto his wife, and they two shall be one flesh. This is a great mystery: but I speak concerning Christ and the church. Nevertheless let every one of you in particular so love his wife even as himself; and the wife see that she reverence her husband." Ephesians 5:22-33

A somewhat parallel passage, Colossians 3:18-19, refers to husbands and wives in the plural; however, it is clear that Paul is addressing all husbands and wives among the Colossian believers and is not suggesting that a husband might have multiple wives. If polygamy were allowed, the entire illustration of Christ's relationship with His bride (the church) and the husband-wife relationship fall apart.[1]

God's intention was not for polygamy when He created Adam and Eve, but He seemed to allow it to solve a problem that arose due to the sinfulness of man. However, it is not the ideal. Because in marriage a man and a woman become one flesh, and because of the need for oneness and harmony in marriage and the lack of any need for polygamy, it is our belief that polygamy does not honor God, and it is not God's design for marriage.[2]

THE STATUS OF WOMEN IN CHRISTIANITY

Women, like men, are made in the image of God and, like men, are honored or censured in the Bible as they respond with faith or with unbelief to their Creator. In the New Testament, we can see how Jesus' treatment of women is a perfect example of His loving and compassionate attitude. His attitude to women was almost revolutionary as He treated them with unusual respect. He was filled with compassion for the disreputable woman who entered the banquet in the home of Simon the Pharisee. When she washed His feet with her oil and tears and wiped His feet using her hair, Jesus Christ, knowing who she was, received her sorrow for her sins and her vow to love and serve Him with all that she was and had. In Luke's account in chapter 7:48-50, Jesus said to her:

> "And He said unto her, Thy sins are forgiven. And they that sat at meat with Him began to say within themselves, Who is this that forgiveth sins also? And He said to the woman, Thy faith hath saved thee; go in peace."

Jesus showed respect for Mary of Bethany when she poured expensive perfume on Him. She understood that Christ had to be crucified, and so she set out to prepare His body for the tomb. He defended her in front of His disciples, who could not understand why this woman would waste such an expensive perfume on Him. He glorified her act saying:

> "Verily I say unto you, Wheresoever this gospel shall be preached in the whole world, there shall also this, that this woman hath done, be told for a memorial of her." Matthew 26:13

His promise is eternal; today we continue reading about Mary and what she did because of her love for Jesus.

Jesus honored women by bringing them to witness His resurrection. Mary Magdalene was the first to witness His resurrection. He charged women to inform the disciples that His body was no longer in the tomb, which shows the importance and respect that Jesus held for the women in the Bible.

There are numerous verses in the Bible that discuss the role and status of Christian women, as in such books as 1 Corinthians, 1 Timothy, Ephesians, Colossians, 1 Peter, 1 Timothy, and Titus, However, after reading some of these verses, it is easy to jump to the conclusion that Paul possessed a rather harsh attitude toward women, but we need to understand the context in which these verses were written. For example, in 1 Corinthians 14:33-38, Paul's words are subject to debate. It has been suggested that Paul was addressing a particular problem in the Corinthian Church, specifically speaking of a group of women who were disruptive.

God made woman a man's helper, meaning that she is not inferior to him, but rather there to be his support. In addition, a woman, who is a godly mother, is given high respect in Christianity, as the following verses show:

> "Her children arise up, and call her blessed; her husband also, and he praiseth her." Proverbs 31:28

Submission to our husbands should not be misconstrued as being a slave; however, we need to first acknowledge our God-given roles. Husbands and wives are to be mutually respectful and submissive to each other as we read in Ephesians 5:21, where both men and women are to submit themselves "one to another in the fear of God."

At the same time, God has established a line of authority in an effort to maintain order in a household. Paul writes:

"Now I want you to realize that the head of every man is Christ, and the head of the woman is man, and the head of Christ is God." 1 Corinthians 11:3.

We know that Christ is not inferior to God, just as a wife is not inferior to her husband. God recognizes, however, that without submission to authority, there is no order. The husband's responsibility as the head of his household is to love his wife as he loves his own self, in the same sacrificial way that Christ loved the church (Ephesians 5:25-29).

As followers of Christ, we women must rejoice in Him and thank Him for making us Christ-like women and for giving us the honor of being called His daughters. We must live our lives as Christ wants us to live them rather than trying to meet worldly expectations. We must honor our husband as the head of the family and help him to maintain the authority that is given to him by Christ. We need to be witnesses of God without trying to prove to anyone that we are perfect, but instead, we need to let the Lord work in our lives. He will surely give us grace and wisdom to walk in Him and follow His footsteps (Proverbs 31:31). In a Christian marriage, as a covenant, the most important word should be "we," and the least important word should be "I."

End Notes

1) www.gotquestions.org/polygamy/why did God allow polygamy/bigamy in the Bible.

2) Ibid

Chapter 9
The Final Answer Is?

THE COMPROMISED CHRIST
OF THE QUR'AN

In the opening chapters, we said that Muslims have a goal to attempt to spread Islam vigorously. One way to achieve this goal is to lure Western women into marriages and then convert them. Consequently, the children of these marriages will be raised in the Muslim faith. To understand this is very difficult for a young woman when she is head over heels in love with her Muslim man.

I have met several women here who have either dated or married Muslims. Some of these women are attending church on a regular basis or, after a long period of absence, have recently re-joined the congregation. When I questioned them about their attraction to their Muslim boyfriend or husband, the answer was always simple: they were certain that he loved them and that Islam had a lot in common with Christianity, especially when talking about Christ. These women claimed that their lover/ex-husband explained to them that the Qur'an has much to say about Christ, His virgin birth, His miracles, and the fact that He is a prophet.

It is true that the Qur'an DOES talk about Christ, who is called "Isa," son of Mary, as 'Apostle of Allah' (Sura 3:49), 'Servant of Allah' (Sura 19:30). He was born of a Virgin

(Sura 19:20). He was holy and faultless (Sura 19:19). He raised the dead and healed the sick (Sura 5:113). Jesus Christ is also mentioned in Sura 4:171, Sura 19:21, Sura 21:91, etc. Do all of these notations sound very convincing? After reading so much about Christ in the Qur'an, what woman would not fall for a Muslim's assertion that Islam and Christianity have so much in common that she can see no reason why she should not convert?

But deception (Al-Taqiyya), a powerful tool, is often used by Muslims all over the world. In fact, deception and how to deceive are part of Islam's teachings. It is true that a Muslim respects Christ as a prophet, but they do not and cannot imagine Him being superior to Muhammad. They will never claim that Jesus is the Son of God; to say so would be 'shirk', which means the establishment of an equal partner with Allah. This is a terrible sin and considered to be idolatry. Furthermore, a Muslim does not believe that Christ died on the Cross for our sins. They believe that another man died in His place, and He was merely lifted up to Heaven. Muslims believe that Allah would not allow one of his prophets to die a death of disgrace.

> "And (for) their saying, 'Indeed, we have killed the messiah, Jesus, the son of Mary, the messenger of Allah.' And they did not kill him, nor did they crucify him; but another was made to resemble him to them. And indeed, those who differ over it are in doubt about it. They have no knowledge of it except the following of assumption. And they did not kill him, for certain." Qur'an 4:157

When a woman thinks that Muslims have knowledge about Christ, she believes that she will be equally yoked.

Marriage to a Muslim man seems to come with very few problems, as both husband and wife believe in one god, who is Allah, and in Christ. This concept somehow causes the woman to reason that her marriage will be an equal partnership and that she will be loved, protected, and respected in the marriage. She cannot know how mistaken this concept is and how unequal the partnership will become. Her life may have been based on a loving, compassionate God, but that is about to change once she becomes involved with a Muslim.

MUHAMMAD AND HIS TREATMENT OF WOMEN

Muhammad was a warrior who fought seventy-four battles and was considered ruthless against those who fought him and stole from him. A striking instance of his cruelty occurs in Bukh Sahibu aari, where Muhammad killed several tribesmen to whom he had offered hospitality. These tribesmen robbed him of several camels, killed one of his men, and then fled. To take revenge, the prophet sent some of his men after them, seizing them and returning them to Medina. Muhammad ordered their hands and feet cut off as punishment for the theft, and he had their eyes pulled out.

Muhammad also had a number of volunteer executioners, who were competent and ready to kill anyone at any time, as their prophet commanded. On another occasion, he sent his disciple, Abdul ibn Oneis, into the camp of a rival tribal chief, Sufyan ibn Khalid, to assassinate him and bring back his head, which the disciple did, throwing the bloody trophy at the feet of the prophet on his return to camp. When his enemy's head was thrown at his feet, Muhammad exclaimed that the dead man's head was more acceptable to him than the best camel in Arabia.[1]

Another example is of the killing of the poetess named Asma Bint Marwan, who disagreed with Muhammad and instigated people against him. One night as she was asleep, surrounded by her children with one child still suckling, his follower Umarb Adiya al Khatmi thrust his sword in her chest till it pierced through to her back. The next day when he offered prayers with Muhammad, Muhammad asked him, "Have you slain the daughter of Marwan?"[2]

Muhammad not only took pleasure in killing people who opposed him, but he also indulged in collecting beautiful women and adding them to his harem. He had eleven wives and three concubines, although some sources give a different number.

According to Bukhara in the Hadith, Muhammad sometimes had sex with all of his wives in a single night, boasting that he had been given the power of forty men.[3]

One of Muhammad's eleven wives, Zainab, was the divorced wife of his adopted son, Zaid. Muhammad decided to marry her after accidently seeing her scantily clad and exclaiming, "Gracious Lord! How dost thou turn the hearts of men?" Zainab understood the message and told her husband. Zaid officially divorced her by pronouncing three times, "I divorce you," while facing toward Mecca. Zainab was now free to marry her previous father-in-law.[4] Note that Muhammad had to receive a special revelation from Allah for permission to do this, as it was against law and custom for a man to marry his son's wife.

When Muhammad had triumphed in battle and slain the enemy, he would take possession of the plunder, capturing the women and children to be used as slaves. It was at that point that the women were distributed among his followers for their sexual pleasures. Of course, Muhammad would keep the most beautiful women for his own pleasures. One such case was Safiya, a seventeen-year-old Jewish woman, who had been captured during a raid on Kheibar. Safiya was the daughter of Chief Huyeiy lbn Akhtab of the Banu Nadir Jewish tribe of Madina. Her husband Kinana, a young Jewish leader, was tortured and killed.

"The apostle occupied the Jewish forts one after the other, taking prisoners as he went. Among these were Safiya, the wife of Kinana, the Kheiber chief, and two female cousins; the apostle chose Safiya for himself. The other prisoners were distributed among the Muslims. Bilal brought Safiya to the apostle, and passed the bodies of several Jews on the way. Safiya's female companions lamented and strewed dust on their heads. When the apostle of Allah observed this scene, he said, 'Remove these she-devils from me.' But he ordered Safiya to remain, and threw his reda (cloak) over her. So the Muslims knew he had reserved her for his own. The apostle reprimanded Bilal, saying, 'Hast thou lost all feelings of mercy, to make women pass by the corpses of their husbands?' Safiya was then taken to Muhammad's tent. He wanted to have sex with her on that very night, only hours after torturing to death her husband"[5] (Ibn Ishaq p.766).

Safiya was not the only victim of Muhammad's lustful eyes. The story of Juwairiya and Rayhanah is also well known in Islam. It has been recorded in several Hadiths that Muhammad did not prohibit his followers from having sex with slave women. Muslims consider Abu Dawood to be highly accurate and factual.

> "Yahya related to me from Malik from Humayd ibn Qays al-Makki that a man called Dhafif said that Ibn Abbas was asked about coitus interruptus (sic). He called a slave-girl of his and said, 'Tell them.' She was embarrassed. He said, 'A man does not practice coitus interruptus (sic) with a free woman unless she gives permission. There is no harm in practicing coitus interruptus (sic) with a slave-girl without her permission. Someone who has another's slave-girl as a wife does not practice coitus interruptus (sic) with her unless her people give him permission."[6] Abu Dawood, 29, 29.32.100

Truth is always powerful. Do not be fooled with what Muslims tell about Muhammad. They claim that he was an exemplary man, a prophet. If he claimed to be a prophet and the perfect man, then he should have lived a pious life. Rather than killing people to spread Islam, he should have reached them with unconditional love. To truly understand your role in Islam, you have to have insight into the teachings of Muhammad and how Muslims everywhere view his teachings and life as the perfect example that they should follow as closely as possible. His attitude and opinion about women can be further seen in several Hadiths taken from Sahih-Al-Bukhari, which is considered to be the most authentic book after Qur'an. For example we read:

> Muhammad asked some women, "Isn't the witness of a woman equal to half that of a man?" The

women said, "Yes." He said, "This is because of the deficiency of the woman's mind." Bukhari Vol 3:826

Muhammad continues in different Hadiths that:

"Bad omen is in the woman, the house and the horse…" Muhammad mentions that, "After me I have not left any affliction more harmful to men than women…" Yet, another verse tells how Muhammad's wife Aisha feels degraded, "The things which annul prayers were mentioned before me and (those were a dog, a donkey, and a woman…) Bukhari Vol 7:30, 7:33 and Vol 1:9 #490

Unfortunately, many women living in the Muslim world, who realize the truth and want to escape, find all exits closed. They are not allowed to question Muhammad's views, as Islam allows no criticism. They suffer in silence, unseeing and unseen.

"JESUS CHRIST—THE SON OF GOD:" THE GREATEST GIFT

Many times I remind myself that Christ died for me and for my sins; when I think of this, my heart starts racing. Jesus is the Lamb of God, who takes away the sins of the world. By dying on the Cross, He showed how much He loves us, not only for those who love and believe in Him, but for those who killed Him. In Luke 23:24, Jesus prays: "Father, forgive them; for they do not know what they are doing." His message is a message of love and peace, teaching us how to love our enemies and to pray for those who persecute us for His namesake. (Matthew 5:44).

For many Christian women living in Muslim countries, this prayer is very real. For many women living with Muslim husbands, if they learn of Jesus, His love comes as a wonderful freedom as they learn their value in the sight of God.

He came to heal the sick: even a woman who was suffering from a terrible disease, which in those days would have been very embarrassing. Yet, she had faith that Jesus had the power to heal her and courageously reached out just to touch Him.

> "And behold, a woman which was diseased with an issue of blood for twelve years, came behind Him and touched the hem of his garment: For she said within herself, if I may touch His garment, I shall be whole. But Jesus turned himself about, and when He saw her, He said, 'Daughter, be of good comfort, thy faith hath made thee whole.' And the woman was made whole from that hour."
> Matthew 9:20-22

He has the power to forgive our sins and heal infirmities, which are a result of sin. Jesus' words are words of forgiveness:

> "Therefore I tell you, her many sins have been forgiven, as her great love has shown. But whoever has been forgiven little loves little."

Here he is speaking of a sinful woman, whose anointing of Jesus was in response to Jesus' message of compassions for sinners. There is humility, devotion, and courage in this woman's act of service. Her action speaks volumes. Jesus knew her reputation, but He was interested in what the woman could become through the grace of God. He confirms that her love had come from being forgiven. She knew He had the power and authority to forgive (Luke 7:47).

He has power over Satan and his demons. What about Mary Magdalene who had seven demons cast out? Jesus attributes the infirmity to Satan, and this is evident that the demons are afraid of Him, demonstrating His authority over Satan.

> "And it came to pass afterward, that He went throughout every city and village, preaching and shewing the glad tidings of the kingdom of God: and the twelve were with Him, And certain women, which had been healed of evil spirits and infirmities, Mary called Magdalene, out of whom went seven devils." Luke 8:1-2

Again we see His power over the demons in the following verses from the Bible:

> "Then was brought unto Him one possessed with a devil, blind, and dumb: and He healed him, insomuch that the blind and dumb both spake and saw. And all the people were amazed, and said, Is not this the Son of David? But when the Pharisees heard it, they said, This fellow doth not cast out devils, but by Beelzebub the prince of the devils. And Jesus knew their thoughts, and said unto them, Every kingdom divided against itself is brought to desolation; and every city or house divided against

itself shall not stand: And if Satan cast out Satan, he is divided against himself; how shall then his kingdom stand? And if I by Beelzebub cast out devils, by whom do your children cast them out? therefore they shall be your judges. But if I cast out devils by the Spirit of God, then the kingdom of God is come unto you. Or else how can one enter into a strong man's house, and spoil his goods, except he first bind the strong man? and then he will spoil his house." Matthew 12:22-29

He did not come to condemn us. How Jesus longed to forgive and to point a woman to a better way. In contrast to the stonings of Islam, Jesus confronted her with her sin, showed her that she could be forgiven, and put her on the right path.

"And the scribes and Pharisees brought unto Him a woman taken in adultery; and when they had set her in the midst, They say unto Him, Master, this woman was taken in adultery, in the very act. Now Moses in the law commanded us, that such should be stoned: but what sayest thou? This they said, tempting Him, that they might have to accuse Him. But Jesus stooped down, and with His finger wrote on the ground, as though He heard them not. So when they continued asking Him, He lifted up Himself, and said unto them, He that is without sin among you, let him first cast a stone at her. And again He stooped down, and wrote on the ground. And they which heard it, being convicted by their own conscience, went out one by one, beginning at the eldest, even unto the last: and Jesus was left alone, and the woman standing in the midst. When Jesus had lifted up Himself, and saw none but the woman, He said unto her, Woman, where are those thine accusers? hath no man condemned thee? She said, No man, Lord. And Jesus said unto her, Neither do I condemn thee: go, and sin no more." John 8:3-11

In contrast to the compassion and mercy shown by Jesus to the woman caught in adultery, Muhammad instructs that an adulterer or adulteress be put to death by stoning. One of Muhammad's followers, Abdullah bin Umar, said: "The Jew brought the prophet a man and a woman from amongst them who have committed (adultery) illegal intercourse. He ordered both of them to be stoned (to death), near the place of offering the funeral prayers beside the mosque."[7]

How different was the response of Jesus who is always ready to offer forgiveness to those who come to Him.

The New Testament is filled with astonishing miracles and healings that Christ performed. Even today, people around the world are being healed in His name. Millions are receiving the blessed gift of salvation and being set free; multitudes are being fed. In His name, the message of the Gospel is being proclaimed. One must ask, why are miracles, healing, and deliverance from demons not being done in the name of Muhammad, Buddha, or any other prophet's name? The answer is simple: because no one has been given the authority to do so. John tells us that Jesus is the name above all names (John 17:1-5).

Many books have been written about Jesus Christ, but for me, what matters most is what He has done for me and what He means to me. With humility and overflowing joy, I declare that His Grace is sufficient for me. He still opens the eyes of the blind, opens the hearts of the lost, gives us abundant life, and promises eternal life to those who believe in Him. While on earth, He had the authority to walk on water and calm the tumultuous storm, as He today can calm the storm in our hearts and lives. He is the Way, the Truth, and the Life and now sits at the right hand of His Father on high.

You may have heard this saying before. However, my heart wishes to say this again. At home, I have a small, beautiful wooden plank. On it is engraved: I asked Jesus, "How much do you love me? And He looked at me and said, 'This much,' and He stretched out His arms and died." How many Muslim women would be amazed and thrilled to know this for themselves? He not only carried the cross for me, but also for the whole world. And He still waits for people to come to Him and be blessed by His saving Grace.

As Christians, we are called to be great witnesses. We are to show forth Christ, not only to Muslims, but also to all the lost living among us. People need to know that Christ is waiting for them with His arms stretched wide, and they need to know that, if they accept Him as their Savior, eternity awaits them. However, this has to be done wisely.

> "Behold, I send you forth as sheep in the midst of wolves; be ye therefore wise as a serpent, and harmless as doves." Matthew 10:16

If we do not wake up now and understand the threat of Islam as it is knocking on our door, then it will be too late. It is one thing to be tolerant and another thing to let someone whose ideas and goals are completely different from yours—and, indeed, destructive toward yours—to invade your home and country.

This threat of invasion is currently happening in Europe and other countries around the world. As long as the Muslim population remains at one percent in any country, they will be regarded as a peace-loving minority and not a threat. We currently find approximately a 1.5 percent Muslim population residing in Italy, 1.8 percent in Norway, 1.5 percent in Australia, 1.9 percent in Canada, one to two percent in China, and one percent in the United States.[8]

Even though Muslims represent a mere one percent of the U.S. population, they are vigorously working to bring more and more Muslims into Western countries. They are doing it quietly so that we are not even aware of what is happening in our neighborhoods. They want to become a dominant force in our culture. As a way of achieving this outcome, our children, especially our daughters, are becoming victims of the charms of male Muslims. So far, these attempts at wooing our young girls have been successful as they strive to achieve their goals.

In the West, Islam is considered a peaceful religion and a peaceful way of life. Although some are waking up to the Islamic goal of the whole world coming under Muslim rule, many in the West are still asleep. Many Christian parents are asleep, too, as their daughters are being won by Muslim young men and are becoming part of Dawah, the great Muslim mission to take over those parts of the world still free from Muslim domination.

MY FRIEND'S CONFESSION

A dear friend of mine forwarded an email of her sister, Paula, sharing a very sobering story about her rooster that truly made me stop and think about Christ and our promises to Him. Maybe the story will affect you in the same way that it did me.

Paula awoke one morning to silence: no rooster crowing in her backyard! She was filled with a dread that the rooster might be dead. Her family had been less than adept at raising animals. Probably seventy or more chickens had died because the chicken coup had been placed in the woods! Foxes and weasels had feasted on many of the helpless chicks. But there hadn't been a massacre in quite a while, at least for nine months, because of a big, boisterous, chesty rooster (hatched in Paula's coop), who had protected the hens.

Sadly, she found him dead one morning. This is how it happened. Paula confessed that she had let him out the previous morning to eat some bugs and grass, but she had forgotten to shut him back into the pen at night. She had forgotten to do this a few weeks back, too, but somehow, all had survived. This time, though, she remembered the open gate at one o'clock in the morning.

So, as she related the story, she had wrestled with her conscience. Should she go out there and shut the gate? The chickens could all be dead in the morning. But she remembered that they had survived the last time that mistake had been made. Also, Paula was afraid to go out there in the dark. Her husband was exhausted, so she could not ask him to go with her. So she decided to just pray in the dark of her room.

Sometime in the night, Paula said she heard a small voice saying, "I gave you charge of the chickens. You protect them." However, she was very tired, and she rolled over and asked God to do it for her. Her sleep was agitated, and when her husband went out to check on the chickens early the next morning, he said that their rooster had not survived an epic battle. The valiant rooster had successfully protected all of the hens; they were indeed all accounted for. When Paula and her son went out later to pay their respects to the noble rooster, they saw his battleground with feathers everywhere, and the rooster was still flinching in the corner, as dead chickens often do.

As Paula's love and admiration grew stronger for the beloved rooster, she thought of our Lord:

"Greater love has no one than this, than to lay down one's life for his friends." John 15:13

Her family sadly buried their courageous animal with some kind words and shed a few tears because they will miss their proud rooster. Paula said:

"But I hope that I, in particular, don't miss the glaring message in the loss of that rooster. Many of MY friends walk in darkness and are unaware of lurking dangers, and yet I sleep. The gate of darkness is open in their lives, and many evils await the opportunity to enter. I have the protection of God's light to shed on any lurking evil, but I must be willing to get out of bed and tread through the darkness. I need to overcome my laziness and fear in order to help my friends live. Perhaps if I can learn and apply this lesson to my life, our rooster will not have been lost in vain. 'Greater love has no one than this, than to lay down one's life for his friends.'"

How true it is that we do not want to leave our comfort zones to reach out to people who are hurting. We need to take courage and share what Christ has done for us. So many young people today are vulnerable to subtle attacks from the enemy; false teachings are everywhere. If we do not reach out to these sons and daughters, perhaps other religions will try to fill that vacuum in their lives. Islam is already aggressively targeting our children, trying to seize them and take them to the valley of death. We need to understand that we are in a spiritual war that can only be fought by the power of prayer.

"For we wrestle not against flesh and blood, but against principalities, against powers, against the rulers of the darkness of this world, against spiritual wickedness in high places." Ephesians 6:12

FINALE

You need to share what you know about Islam with your children so that they will make wise decisions. Encourage them to make decisions based on the wisdom given to us in the Bible, rather than on hatred and fear. Some of my friends have told me that I should not be sharing graphic details concerning the treatment of Muslim women while my eleven-year-old daughter is present in a group. They tell me that discussing the treatment of women, including the beatings and the rapes, is too violent for children to hear. I have listened to this objection and know that, by God's grace, my children will be making their own decisions within the next few years. I want them to know very clearly that we must not "be yoked together with unbelievers."

I know of several cases where women have married Muslim men, and the marriages ended in divorce. In the beginning, their love for each other seemed ideal. However, the relationship did not remain ideal for very long. Several women are still hurting because they are unable to see their children anymore; for others, the scars of painful memories are buried deep within. Sadly, the consequences of passion overriding rational judgment have become all too common in these situations. Young women need to be made aware of the dangers of dating or of eventually marrying a Muslim man. Christian women need to know that once they marry into the Muslim world, they may be asked to renounce Christ by their husbands and to embrace the Islamic doctrine. Are they truly willing to take that step?

A Muslim man, strong in his beliefs, will not compromise his faith because of his marriage to a western woman. Once married, a woman will find her entire life ruled by the honor and shame principle. The freedom that she enjoys in her free country and has taken for granted all of her life will be stripped away forever. If you are concerned that this may be happening in your community, then it is necessary for all believers (church leaders and parents) to begin to educate the young about faith. Teach your children the truth about other religions, pointing out the pitfalls of each. Educate yourselves in order to fully educate your children. At the age of eighty-two, my mother still asks me if I pray and teach my children from the Scripture. There have been times when I said, "Mom, why do you always ask me that?" and she replies, "As a mother, it is my responsibility to remind you to remain faithful to the Lord, and I will do what He has asked me till my last breathe on this earth."

Well-informed children will be strengthened in their faith and will be able to stand strong as Christian believers.

There is much documented evidence that women are ill-treated by the men of Islam. Muslim women do not complain because they do not know any better. Even if they were aware that there is another and better way of life, they do not question the prophet Muhammad and the word of Allah as spoken in the Qur'an. Thus, this lack of knowledge, combined with fear and oppression, is keeping these women in a never-ending cycle of abuse.

At a very early stage of my career, I met my colleague, Huma, who later became a good friend of mine. She belonged to a very wealthy family and was indeed a very pretty girl. Her father married her off, and after one year of her marriage, she returned back to her father's home because she wanted to get a divorce. I met her again two years after her marriage. As I had attended her wedding, which was indeed a very extravagant one, I was wondering what made her take such a huge step of seeking a divorce. This is what she told me. A few weeks after her marriage, her husband started beating her. This was a result of her questioning why he was coming home late at nights with lipstick stains on his shirts. She would complain to her mother-in-law, who in return would tell her to mind her own business. She was barricaded in, not just in her in-laws' home, but also confined in her bedroom. She was not allowed to meet friends and family. When she tried to escape or became angry about her treatment, her mother-in-law would set hungry dogs on her, and her husband would beat her with hose pipes leaving her bruised. Finally, after a year, she was rescued by her brother. She felt good when she shared how free she felt, as if flying on the wing of an eagle.

At last, I asked a foolish question knowing that it would take her a long time to recover from that trauma: "Huma, do you think you would want to marry again?"

She leaned forward and whispered a very daring answer in my ear, "If I marry again, this time I will marry a Christian man who will love me like he loves His Christ." Her eyes and smile were full of hope.

Today there are many Muslim women, like Huma, who are daring and just need hope—the hope of the Living God who will never leave them nor forsake them. They are willing to hear the story of that amazing love of the King who died for them.

If you feel burdened by the Lord to reach out to a Muslim woman or any woman involved in a Muslim relationship, your first step will be to go before the Lord in prayer. Only through His guidance, wisdom, and opportunity will your ministry be successful. Remember, it is not you, but He will work through you. You are there only to plant the seed; the rest is in His Hands. Allow the Holy Spirit to work through your life and the life of the one you are trying to reach, using you as His vessel.

It is interesting to note that, within Islamic culture, women only speak to other women, and men only speak to other men. As you build a relationship with the women you are trying to reach for the Lord, keep in mind that they come from a culture that is quite different from the West. Sacrifice, patience, perseverance, and unconditional love are the stepping stones to winning a Muslim woman for Christ. Also, be reminded that they are observing you very closely. They want to see if you are the living example of Jesus Christ and not just preaching Him. Also, we are not called to fit it in, but to stand out. Unlike on the television show, "Who Wants to be a Millionaire," we have only one Lifeline, and that is the blood of Christ. Are you willing to share this Lifeline and plant the seed in someone's heart today?

Jesus walked the earth, and through His example in the Gospels, the status of women was elevated. We are no longer enslaved by the law, but we have been set free by the shedding of the blood of our Savior. I often think to myself, "I am the daughter of the High King. Just imagine how much I am loved by Him." We can joyfully fulfill our God-given responsibilities as daughters, sisters, mothers, and grandmothers. He is the God of love, and we are made in His image and likeness. He has bestowed honor upon us.

THE RIPPLE EFFECT

This, I believe, is not the end of the book, but the beginning of a new chapter—a chapter that you will write. Let this knowledge start a ripple effect. We should recognize that, as women, God has called us for a much deeper purpose, and that is to reach out to the dying world with the Good News of who Jesus Christ is. What God requires of us is our hearts and our availability, and then He is able to do more through us. God made the word "Love" a verb, and this action was demonstrated through His greatest act of sacrifice—His gracious gift of His Son who was, is, and will be present to everyone in every tribe and nation (Titus 2:11-14, Rev. 5:9-10).

> "For God so loved the world that He gave His only begotten Son, that whoever believes in Him should not perish but have everlasting life." John 3:16

As women, the joy, freedom, relationship, knowledge, and love given to us by Jesus Christ so freely is not to be hidden in the closets of our hearts, but we are expected to share it with others. There were only twelve simple men who touched people with the love of Christ and changed their world. Let us, as women today, touch someone's world, too, not with what we can do, but what Christ can do through us. In the world of fear and oppression, people need to know that JESUS IS THE PRINCE OF PEACE.

I pray that God will bless you all immensely and give you the boldness to do what He has called you to do and to show women everywhere that Jesus loves and values them, that He can give them freedom and purpose, and that He can assure them of salvation and their place in Heaven. Amen.

> "Regardless of what the future holds for us, our families, our church, and our world, may we have the joy of knowing that we defended His Word and lived His Word for His glory and the sake of those He has chosen."[9]

End Notes

1) Paul Fregosi, Jihad, Chap 4, Pg 46.

2) Ibn Ishaq. Pg 675-676.

3) Peter Hammond: Slavery, Terrorism and Islam. The Historical roots and contemporary threat, Chap 8, The oppression of women in Islam.

4) Paul Fregosi, Jihad, Chap 4, Pg 46.

5) http://www.faithfreedom.org/challenge/rapist.htm.

6) www.sykkuvab-country.com/Islam/rape. Muhammad: A rapist. By Ali Sina.

7) Sahih Bukhari 2:23:413.

8) Synopsis of Islam and how it works, adapted from Dr. Peter Hammond: Slavery, Terrorism and Islam.

9) Ken Ham, Already gone.

References

Slavery, Terrorism and Islam: The Historical Roots and Contemporary Threat, by Dr. Peter Hammond, Christian Liberty Books, South Africa, 2005

Unveiling Islam, by Dr Ergun Caner and Dr.Emir Caner, Kregel Publications, Michigan, 2002.

Out of the Crescent Shadows, by Dr Ergun Caner and Dr Emir Caner, New Hope Publishers, Birmingham, Alabama, 2003.

Does Christianity Squash Women? A Christian looks at womanhood, by Rebecca Jones, Broadman &Holman Publishers, Nashville Tennesse, 2005.

Mirage, The Love Language of Islam! Wake up America ...Before it's too Late, by David Ibrahim, Advancing Native Missions Publishers, Charlottesville, Virginia, 2010.

Already Gone, Why your kids will quit Church and what you can do to stop it, by Ken Ham & Britt Beemer with Todd Hillard, Master Books Publishers, Green Forest, Arizona, 2009.

Raising Godly Children in an Ungodly World, Leaving a Lasting Legacy, by Ken Ham and Steve Ham, Master Books Publishers, Green Forest, Arizona, 2006.

What He Must Be...if He Wants to Marry my Daughter, by Voddie Baugham Jr, Crossway Publishers, Wheaton, Illinois, 2009.

A Father's Reward, Raising your children to walk in the truth, by Phil Downer, Eternal Impact Publishers, Signal Mountain, Tennessee, 1998, 2004, 2007.

Jihad in the West, by Paul Fregosi, Prometheus Books Publishers, 1998.

Why Christian Woman Convert to Islam, by Rosemary Sookhdeo, Isaac Publishing,

Who is Allah?, G.J.O .Moshay, Fireliners Internatioanl (AKA Jijor-ho Publishing Corp.,) Ibadan, Nigeria, West Africa, 1990.

Women In Islam, Equal or Inferior, by Dr . Sameh, Oasis Publishers,1997.